SUGBO

King Macachor

Revised Edition

King Macachor

ISBN-13: 978-1519702203
ISBN-10: 1519702205

DEDICATION

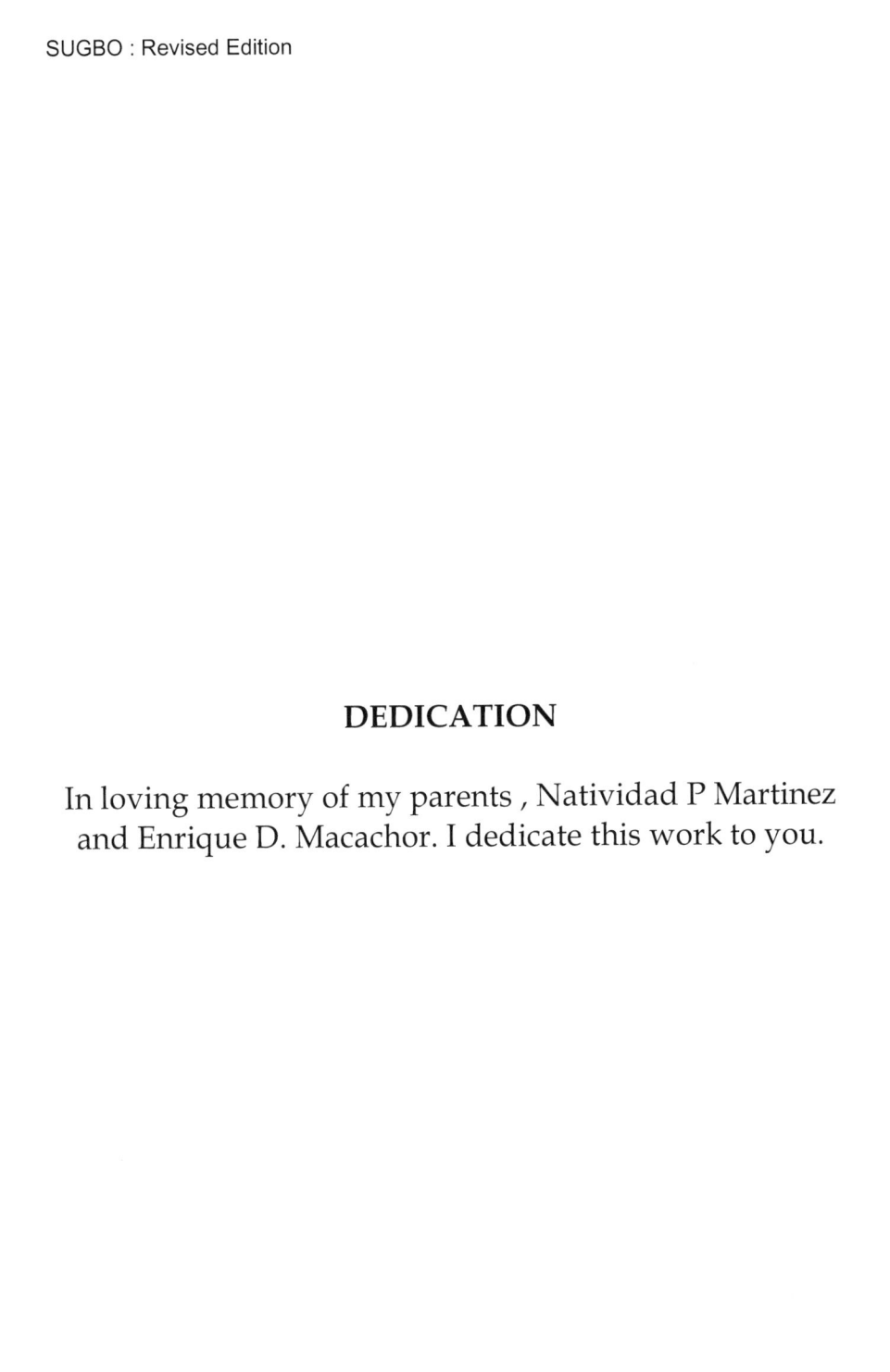

In loving memory of my parents , Natividad P Martinez and Enrique D. Macachor. I dedicate this work to you.

King Macachor

PRINTED BY

CreateSpace

ACKNOWLEDGMENT

I am grateful to all those people who encouraged me to create this work, my family, my editor, my close friends and all my students.

King Macachor

CHAPTER 1

It was in one of those tranquil evenings when they were seated in the garden on a swing among the fragrant flowers, Ilang-ilang and her great-grandma Hana. Cool breeze from the forest brushed lightly on their faces to cheer them up from the summer heat. Up in the sky, the full moon's sad contour dimmed gradually, cowering itself behind the clouds. Great-grandma looked up and sighed, traces of sadness fading from the moonlight. Life had been good but what remaining happiness would it offer when the love of her life had been gone to share it with? Tears shone in her eyes.

"My dear child, I'm sorry but I can't hold myself from remembering and feeling sad. My memory of your Lolo Amir is still fresh. It's as if he lingers around, beside me, everywhere, right here with us."

"Poignant memories live with us, Lala."

"Indeed they do. They free our soul to cherish all those happy moments we had, reliving every bit of them. Though to reminisce is liberating yet it made me sadder," Lala Hana sighed deeply.

"Being sad is fleeting, you feel it now and when you let it go I believe it will slowly die out. Lala, I want you to be happy. Please don't be sad! Now here, what good is it if you don't share it with me? Let's talk about Lolo. Tell me your story, please."

"Our life together had never been so meaningful, my dear," Lala Hana said, wiping the tears from her cheek with a handkerchief.

"I'm all ears, Lala Hana," Ilang-ilang assured her great-grandma, with eyes glowing with interest.

"Here my dear child, let me make myself comfortable a bit and then off we go," her great-grandma sniffed. She sighed again and shifted her legs to gaze beyond, to the looming green forest somewhere in the north of Borneo, where her life had unfolded.

It had all started in the village of Sandakan about eight decades ago. Morning had broken and the sun came up once more in the horizon, gradually spreading its golden rays over the valley, on the forested mountains, then lavishly onto the village. The light glowed brighter and a bit of warmth spread through tawny colored rooftops seeking its way into the homes of the simple folks, then across the night-chilled land. Somewhere among the treetops jays, ravens and robins fluttered off morning dews from their moist wings. Tarsier monkeys squeaked and gibbered. The river flowed calmly towards the great sea.

"`Tock-to-gaock . . .´ roosters heralded its coming with their familiar crowing, a distinct cool sound of early morn which brought comfort to the villagers."

`Amir !´

`Amir !´

"In one of the thatched huts he tossed and turned over, back sweating, in terror, and his heart thumped deeply. Amir heard familiar calls in the background, which tapered into faint inaudible sounds. He dithered, heeding half-heartedly the call from his mother which faded into a dark tunnel, spiralling, and merging into the most inner recesses of his slumber."

"`Give it to me or I'll punch your nose, you little imp,´ boomed the indomitable Limbung, who was overpowering, tormenting him and making his day miserable by scaring him out of his wits."

"His instinct told him to cry knowing that any insensitive hearts, including the bully's, would soften on seeing tears."

"But the softening of the bully's heart lasted for a brief moment. After realizing this trick, he poked his victim's nose and pushed him. Poor Amir was no match to the bigger Limbung. He stood up, fought and fell again. Incidentally one adult intervened and broke them up."

`Hey! Hey! Stop this Limbung. Now go home Amir. Here, take this salt to your mother.´

"`He should learn who the boss is here, you little imp,´ roared Limbung, towering over him with an unbridled snootiness."

"It was the word `imp´ that hurt Amir. This time with a bruised ego, his real tears flowed without restraint. He cried for nothing else but on having lost his pride and self-esteem. He put up a fight but he was no match."

"Who was Limbung, Lala?" asked Ilang-ilang.

"Limbung the imposing, scheming brat of a child who lived a few huts along the river bank on the eastern side was the bully. He was known to be the kingpin of the streets with a reputation for indolence and savagery. Accompanied by his entourage of obeying puppies, he walked the streets of the village pretending to be a Rajah. Among the boys his words was the law."

Ilang-ilang nodded and her great-grandma continued.

"When the poor victim got home his mother saw the mess and was hysterical as to why he had a black bruise around his right eye and his shirt full of mud. He had wanted to hide this from her, but where?"

"`Here, let me see your face. Who did this to you?´ she began investigating."

"`Don't worry *ibu*. Boys are boys. It´s part of growing up,´ said his father, calming her down."

"Lips quivered and eyes brimmed, in short intervals he sobbed. He could barely look at his *ibu*, so he covered them with the back of his hand and wiped the tears with shame."

"`Come with me my son,´ his father slung a comforting arm around his shoulder and led him down to the coop through the creaking bamboo stairs, leaving his mother behind at the *ibuh rumah*. His father opened the lid and slid inside, stirring the animals as they entered. He followed behind. His father picked one cock up with his two hands and showed it to Amir."

"`Look at this beauty. It's tall and its legs and wings are strong. It used to be a helpless fledgling, frail and weak it took me time to nurture it. Now you can see its wings are strong. My little chick can fight any other cocks and it has won me several *sabongs*,´ his father said, stroke its shiny feathers, then blew smoke on its face."

"`Like you, you're still ten, my boy. . . and that skinny body. Wait until you develop your muscles. You'll soon have your time. I don't want to see you beaten once more than today. All I want of you is to be a man, brave and strong.´ He laid it down to mingle with the rest of the flock. It cackled then crowed."

`Now let's have a little talk. Was it Limbung again?´

"Little Amir respectfully nodded, uncertain if he was going to talk or wait for his *ayah* to initiate something, his timidity showed on his face."

"`Stand straight and firm. First, I'd like you to close your hands into a fist and hold them close to your face, this way. Go on. Not too tight. A fist emanates power, an open hand is weak. Now punch straight into the air following me, with your knuckles.´ His father showed him the simple rudiments of hand to hand fighting."

"He did what he was shown and imitated all the punches, blocks and strikes up to the smallest details. All of this sunk into his young mind easily as sponge. His lips widened into a smile and his eyes glowed with excitement, tears gone. The scrawny boy who had lost his self-esteem soon learned there was a way to recover it- to fight with his bare hands, and his confidence improved as time went by."

"Little Amir used to play on the bamboo floor of the *ibuh rumah*. His father's coughing and footsteps going down through the bamboo stairs to the coop were familiar sounds he heard every day. His eyes followed the creaking sound of his footsteps and felt secured he was there alright.

He would peek down through the slits on the floor in between slats to see him blowing smoke on his favourite fighting cock, and the smoke floated up through the slits and into the *ibuh rumah*. The smell of his *lumboy* roll gave him a feeling of security, the assurance he needed his *ayah* was down there among his pets, and that at any time whenever he wants to he would always be right beside him for comfort and protection, though how ephemeral it had been."

"And to tell him his stories which Amir loved, though sometimes repetitious. His *ayah's* mind was as fertile as his invented stories and running out of them was unimaginable. He was a crafty weaver of his experience in life to mould them into his imagination with versatility. Most were about strong men, giants and ogres and about his quest in life. He could take him into the realm of fantasies at the wink of an eye. There's one which he told over and over to remind Amir of another practical lesson in life."

"It went this way, `In one mystifyingly eerie night it was quiet and the air was heavy. Children were restless in their beds and sleep was difficult to find. Folks thought it was an ominous sign for bizarre things to happen.´

`Thirteen year old Hasan was restless. Sleep hardly came to him, so he got out of bed, strode across his room to breathe fresh air through his open window, and looked out, oblivious to the watchful eyes from somewhere. Smoke from rolled lumboy leaves floated in the air towards his direction. His nose tweaked. It came from the acacia tree in front of his hut and the smell beckoned him to come. It was alluring as the songs of the sirens in the islands of Sirenum Scopuli, mesmerizing him. Then he was hypnotized into deep sleep.´

`The following morning he was nowhere to be found and his parents were all over Sandakan worried as to where he had gone. After a futile search he was finally found there at the top of the acacia in one of the branches, sleeping soundly. This happened not only once, in evenings similar to this one but several times over. His parents suspected little on this weird behaviour. It was cool up in the tree to escape from the scorching heat for him to be sleeping away from his room.´

`Neighbours thought otherwise. They poked him questions. His candid explanation was that he was lured by a voice to come and stay at the top of the acacia so that he could cool himself. He obeyed, captivated by the smell of the lumboy smoke. Finally the foreboding sign folks feared came to reality to haunt them forever.´

`Sensing something unusual, the village medicine man was called to find out. He prayed, sprinkled some potions in all corners of their hut and smoked the acacia tree. He said he was driving out bad spirits. But this did not drive the Atgah away.´

`In one of those exceptionally hot days Hasan was nowhere to be found again. He was finally taken by the Atgah.´

`Atgah is scary, tall at 10 feet, dark, hairy and bearded. Having some supernatural powers of invisibility, which he had obtained from the large lumboy roll he smokes, he stalks the village at night to lure young girls to follow him into his realm. After stalking he would relax at the acacia tree smoking a big roll and seen only by the young girls he is enamoured with. He cannot be seen by other people. He will consistently follow her throughout life doggedly to come with him until he succeeds. Nowadays, any young girl who disappears is immediately attributed to Atgah.´"

"`So remember, my boy, not to play near the acacia, venture out into the forest or stray far away from home. Atgah may snatch you and we might not see you again,´ his father reminded him gently."

"`But I'm not a girl, ayah,´ Amir insisted."

"In defence, he retorted that the Atgah which took Hasan would take little boys as well, not only little girls. And if he didn't listen to what he said, punishment would follow. He put lessons in them, lessons to instil in the young mind of the retributions for being stubborn. As always, his *Ayah* was able to manoeuvre his stories craftily."

"After analysing the story and realizing one inconsistent little flaw, the little boy wondered innocently, `huh, if he likes girls then what is he if he likes boys as well? He is hairy and has a beard so he can not be a woman. He could only be a man who likes boys as well.´ This time his *ayah* was caught in his boo-boo again."

"`Does it make any difference if he likes both boys and girls?´ He cut him right away in order to stop the question to progress into a more embarrassing situation, leaving it hanging in the little boy's curious mind."

`After years of absence folks were puzzled by Hasan's unexpected return to Sandakan. He was back but he lost a precious part of his life. When interrogated where he had gone he would say he lost memory of his disappearance.´

`Amir!´

`Amir!´

"It was another call from his mother waking him up from his dream. She opened her windows to let the morning air come rushing in."

"Then one by one window shutters in other huts opened up, to let the first rays penetrate the inner recesses of their homes and folks poured out one after the other. In most homes, still sleepy tots yawned and stretched themselves on matted bamboo floors hoping to prolong their nights a bit longer."

"`Amirrr . . . time to wake up. You'd better be going, son,´ his mother cried out again, shaking him up from his horrid dream, `Tariq must already be awake and waiting for you at the bridge. Go now . . . be back before sundown. And don't forget to bring fish, too,´ she added."

`I'm up, *Ibu*,´ he grumbled.

"Still with clenched fists, he awoke, the dream dissolved and Limbung was gone. Streaks of sweat soaked his neck and back, his eyes squinting. He faintly heard the rushing of water from the river. There was only stillness and the deafening quietness of the dawn in his little room. His mother's voice shook him, and he opened his eyes but closed them back again, indulging a little. His eyelids fluttered knowingly each time his name was called. He stretched his arms and yawned to get out of bed then finally got out of bed, still haunted of the dream he had had. Darkness was fading, and the light of dawn that entered through the open window gave shape to the contours of his familiar room, the chair, the table, the door."

"He stood up and stumbled, groggy with heavy footings, then balanced himself trudging towards the curtain door, drew it apart and stood there at the doorway. Out of his room into the *Ibuh rumah* he groped his way, dragging himself down onto a stool at the table. The cackling down at the coop made him wonder if chickens also sleep. He heard boiling, the aroma wafted through the air, and he sniffed fish soup brewing from the pot."

"None of the village folks had any sense of time, for time was a day or darkness. No seconds, no minutes nor hours. We never had any understanding of the words hectic, be punctual or be late. Amir was never worried about being in a hurry and his life was free of any stress, independent from the ever elusive pressing time. But he knew it was morning because of the cackling and his mother's calling. And it was time to wake up."

"`Here . . . take this before you go. An empty stomach is no good at all,´ said his *ibu*, giving him his steaming hot soup."

"He reached out for the cup and replied, `I would be back before it gets dark, *ibu*. Remember to salt the meat we had the other day,´ muttering his words. He struggled with his soup, blew air to cool it, took a sip then stood up, pacing back and forth. He took another sip and when it was finished he collected his hunting gigs, and decided he was now ready to go."

"`I made *pusó* so that you'll have rice for lunch. It's more than enough for both of you,´ said his mother, after recollecting the utensils to clean them. She moved towards the window to check if the sky was clear then followed him to the door. After kissing him on the cheek she bid him goodbye."

"Amir who was now a full-grown man at nineteen scaled down the bamboo stairs then stepped out onto the dirt road in the direction of Tariq's hut. He flirted with the new day, his head up, his body erect and his brawny muscles heaved when he walked, unmindful of the eyes which were longing for his attention."

"Young girls found him so attractive and his daily routine made them peek through their windows to see him pass. They said his handsome face held by a well-defined jaw made him prominently masculine, complemented equally by a well formed nose and dazzling russet eyes. They also loved to see his long black hair tied around his head with a cloth band, flutter against the wind. Most of all, oh! how they adored his powerfully built body in g-string with a well-defined set of muscles that shone when he moved. All of this was well balanced by his tall height and remarkable bearing. He never wore anything under his feet, but he ran and flitted like a tiger. Unanimously the girls said he stood out on top among the young men in the village."

"On knowing this, did this change him?" inquired Ilang-ilang. "He knew he was attractive, but in spite of this knowledge he was never self-conscious and bigheaded, and still ever so respectful to all the girls he knew were interested on him."

"They also admired his great character. Like anybody else he had no formal education for it was unheard of in this small village and no formal place to learn something yet existed. Its absence however never loosened the very fabric of society. Good manners and correct behaviour was taught at home, and the imaginary line which separated individuals was well respected, never encroached nor transgressed and crime was unheard of. Amir was considered by majority of the folks as an exemplary character, well regarded by his kindness, patience and meekness in spite of the absence of formal learning. Young girls considered him as a gentleman, befitting of someone who had had some royal background or special education in childhood one had obtained from some faraway places."

CHAPTER 2

"Life in Sandakan was simple. This simplicity was manifested by our ways, the means to which we earn our living and how we make use of our time. We never even had any complicated and complex recreations to pass our time. Children played with stones and sticks, and with what little means we had we were nevertheless simply happy."

"Our folks love work. Early birds were already moving around and doing their chores: women folks tended and watered flower gardens while men went down to the coops and talked to their favourite cocks. Some men strewed ear corns on the ground to quick pecking chickens. Outside, pigs and goats roamed around as if nobody owned them and oxs were already tugging poles of bamboos for delivery to new home constructions. Agriculture, fishing or hunting was their means of livelihood and each one was on their way to work. It's time for them to be up and going and to start the day, every day, day in and out. Work was part of living."

`Tock-to-gaock,´ one rooster crowed from one of the coops, then others followed, some in unison.

"Along the river banks stood huts where folks lived, on stilts that stretched towards the sun's rising. Still the same huts that you see nowadays. All of them were made out of nipa frames and coco leaf roofing which sat on upright timbers or bamboo poles driven into the ground to form the foundations. Exactly below from where the family spent the day, which was the *ibuh rumah*, was the coop where domesticated animals were kept. In going down, we took the bamboo narrow steps that led to this coop which was fenced with closed netted rattan strips."

"Amir's father had also been an early riser. He was seen doing things around the house from cleaning the coop to tending his fighting cocks, to carpentering. He built their hut with the crude tools he maintained, within his simple means, albeit he had never learned carpentering. Aside from this he supported his family by fishing and raising domesticated animals. He had a little plot of land at the back of his house where he could pluck cabbages and horse radish anytime he wanted to use them for his soup."

"`Ayah, what do you get from it,´ he overheard his *ibu* nagging his father again. It bothered her so much that she lost thoughtful consideration of his smoking."

`To tell you truthfully, *ibu*, I'm still in the process of learning. Remember my story about Atgah?´

`Don't tell me that excuse again. What do you get from the smoke?´ pressured *ibu*.

`His *lumboy* roll was what gave him the power to become invisible. I smoke because I want to know what power it could give me,´ *Ayah* almost choked coughing again.

`And have you found the answer?´ she exclaimed ironically, arms akimbo.

`So far, I haven't. But I won't stop smoking until I'd find it out,´ *ayah* replied stubbornly still coughing.

`Look at you and your stupidity, you're likely to die smoking before knowing the answers.´ She turned away disgusted.

"This was the same conversation he had heard from his parents over and over. Then one day while little Amir was at the *ibuh rumah* playing, he learned the reason to his *ayah*'s quest in smoking. He could only hear the cackling of the chickens. Strange as it was, he heard no more coughing, nor any sounds from his *ayah*, and the smoke stopped coming so he peered down to see what he was up to. He saw him slumped on the ground facing down and not moving at all, his cocks milling about him. He understood nothing of what this means. A shrill cry from his mother gave out the alarm, and from then on he realized the significance of it all. The security broken, the cord which united them severed. Destiny got a twist for Amir when that fatal stroke snatched his father untimely from him. Change came to knock on his door."

"Poor, Lolo," commented Ilang-ilang.

"Life which had been easy, now was full of challenges. Since then he had to tell himself to cope up, leave his boyhood days behind and assume all the things which his father had to do: to fetch water from the well for his mother, feed the animals at the coop and hunt for food, even to talk with his cocks less the blowing of smoke on their faces. His father's early death hastened his maturity and fortified his mettle. Most of all, he had to assume the responsibility of caring for his surviving mother who was now his whole world. And he loved her dearly."

"His father's departure also changed his outlook in several aspects. He was now more careful in his decisions, taking extra care that his choices were the right ones, and those which would not give him any reasons to regret one day. When it involved choosing a girl he used his head and not his heart. This was the reason he avoided the flirtations of some girls in the village and never revealed to anybody his preference to one girl in particular."

"What occupied his mind and tickled his heart was someone special. He would find himself caught in a net of uplifting thoughts and think about this special one in a daydream."

Ilang-ilang smiled at this part of the story. Then her Lala Hana continued.

"He hated fetching water from the well. He considered it to be burdensome, without any challenge, exceedingly repetitive, monotonous in some ways. But he had to do it because his *ibu* needed water for cooking. One time he failed to fetch water and there was no food on the table, so he had to do it without failure, or he went hungry again, learning his lesson the simplest way."

"Cleaning the coop was another thing. One time he was told by his mother to clean because the smell of their waste went up to the *ibuh rumah*. Since then he had to do it or he would live with the stench. Feeding the animals was not much of a routine for him, though. Being a reticent individual, talking with them in the mornings was a stimulating pastime."

"One evening, at the *ibuh rumah,* Amir was seated on the floor adjusting the stiffness of his bow, cleaning his hunting tools as he usually did, and sharpening them while his *ibu* was sewing her sarong, repairing the seam to preserve it from deterioration. They were silently engrossed into each other's activities when his mother was reminded of *ayah*. She dropped her sewing and went to her room to take out something from a small locked wooden trunk she had been keeping for years. One of those things she found inside was a small blue velvet bag which was closed at the seams with a string. She took it out and her mind wandered to the past when *ayah* was still alive. She turned sentimental and tears shone in her eyes. She held the bag close to her heart and mused at Amir who had grown to be a real man, strong and dependable. Now was the right time, she thought."

"Amir was unmindful of what she was about to say, his eyes following his mother as she came out from her room. `I'd like to tell you something, son, about your father,´ she said, and took a seat beside him. `Remember the pearl he showed you one day? The story that goes around is true. Lore has it that he had been the first in Sandakan to have courageously gone to one of those islands. Going there had never been thought of, yet he had built his raft out of bamboo and crossed the sea. I admire him for his intuitions, to see that out there in those islands he would find something that would change people's impressions on him forever. People thought he was gone forever. I had great hopes he would come back. To their surprise he came back. He brought some golden pearls he got from the sea. He told me to keep them for you until you get to the right age. I have been keeping them so that someday you'd be able to use them. I think now is the right time, Amir,´ she said this, proud of *ayah's* enduring legacy."

"He stopped what he was doing, stretched his arm and reached out for the bag from his *ibu,* eager to see its contents. The excitement at the thought of receiving something from his father surged within him. With hands shaking he loosened the string and poured the contents onto his palm. He was overwhelmed to see them, his eyes glowed at the sight of those golden small roundish thing he had only seen once before. They were iridescent and brilliant. While counting them, with fingers trembling his mind was tossed back to his father's stories. He remembered how he risked his life braving the sea to look for these pearls. He fingered one and rolled it over and over, raised it over his head to watch it glow from the light of the lamp. His eyes twinkled with awe."

`They are beautiful. What should I do with them *ibu*?´

`Keep them. Someday you'll find out their true value. . . unimaginable value. Meantime, just keep them,´ his mother said.

`I saw one of them when ayah showed it to me in his story. I never realized how beautiful it was until now,´ he put them back in the bag one by one, counting them at the same time.

`There are twenty eight here, ibu,´ he said.

"Amir had never forgotten all the stories surrounding the precious pearls. He believed in them with all his heart and mind, including the legends of his great ancestor Kusgan who had embedded one pearl in his wrist to make him strong. This created a certain aura of respect from the village people who learned of their existence, as well."

"The pearls had no immediate use for Amir so far. He knew however that someday exigencies or some conditions would present themselves at the right time for him to learn of their true value. So he thought it would make sense to keep them hidden safe somewhere for the meantime."

"In one of the bamboo post, he had a small hole he had carved with a knife. It was his safe- a small place where he kept all the things he considered with value. He put the velvet bag safely inside and closed it inconspicuously, so that when he found the right time he would come to visit it again."

CHAPTER 3

"His best friend was Tariq. When they were children what he wanted most was to be with him, climbing trees and shooting birds with their slingshots. They would sit side by side all day and practice hitting anything they could think of, such as tree branches, stones or the unlucky birds that strayed off into their path."

"They loved hunting. As they grew older, even if they were looking for food it was always playing for Amir. It brought out the masculinity in him, gave him the chance to enjoy nature, and provided him balance and peace of mind, to the end of taking pleasure in their natural existence aside from being able to hone his skills."

"Tariq's hut stood apart on the other side of the river bounded on the north side by a steep mountain. He crossed the bridge over the river and had walked a bit before reaching it. On the way, Amir surveyed the forest blossoming verdantly like broccolis at the distance. He imagined the monkeys in its midst, playfully jumping from tree to tree, boars fighting heads-on with their sharp tusks, colourful birds feeding their young in their nests, and worms and snakes that lurked and inhabited within its interminable vastness. He looked up and saw swallows going from south to north migrating in thousands overhead."

"He picked a flat stone, balanced it on his palm and with a quick flip of his fingers bounced it onto the top of the water. It glided smoothly three times before it sunk into the bottom. He picked another one and let it bounce four times before proceeding with his walk. This was a game he played privately from time to time. Oftentimes he played it with Tariq and competed with him as to who had the most skips."

"`Tariq . . . the sun's up,´ his voice sprang from mountain to mountain and back, it responded as if it had a life of its own. He loved to hear how it boomed so he shouted again, `Tariqqqqq.´ His voice echoed in the hallowed stillness of dawn."

"Tariq was jolted from sleep. His *ibu* was wrong, thought Amir. Tariq had never gotten up earlier than him."

"Still sleepy eyed, Tariq went sluggishly for his hunting equipment, his mother at his side with his hot drink, while his two younger brothers were still snoring in bed. Then he slipped out, eyes squinting to fight off the daylight that washed his face."

"A jolly good fellow, funny sometimes, Tariq was straightforward in his words but this was balanced by his extra ordinary character. Amir depended on his proficiency with the long bow which he considered to be deadly. He lived with his mother and two younger brothers. Eman was the brainer and the problem solver of the family. Hakim was the youngest and the homely type, who had assumed his father's profession as a carpenter after the latter passed away, now doing all the minor repairs and changes to the family home."

`Why don't we catch fish,´ suggested Amir.

`We go downstream while they're still feeding. Later it would be difficult to find any when they've eaten and hidden among rocks- there should be plenty of them at the end. Then we'd go for the boars after catching enough,´ he continued.

"Tariq went along without saying anything, still brushing off his sleepiness."

"Off they went fishing which they usually do in fair weather - two glaringly opposite individuals, one tall and handsome, the other short but sporty. Then they would go hunt some boars. On the way, they passed fellow villagers who were early on the go: One woman was sweeping her yard to clear it from fallen leaves. On passing, they greeted her a fine morning and she did the same. They also passed a familiar old folk, Mang Andoy, who was already at the top of the coco tree to fetch *tubá*, a tasty local red wine. Another was picking *lumboy* from a tree, they recalled it was season for this dark bluish fruit which resembled berry but tasted sweeter. She offered a handful which they took with them after thanking her. Everybody knew everybody here in the village; they commonly called each other by name."

"The road of the village was unpaved and potholes abound. It was the main road along the side of the river. At the corner, stood the only village store ran by a spinster who was said to have been returned by the Atgah. Neighbours

came to obtain salt, sugar or anything they run out of at home. It was a convenience store and a place for hanging out by loafers. Two benches fronting each other were placed there for them to stand by the whole day, did nothing but talk about nothing. They saw Limbung and four of his friends who were seated on the benches, presumably drinking *tubá* overnight and had not been to bed yet, judging by their looks they were drunk. Amir and Tariq ignored them."

`Limbung's ruddy faced again. I can't understand why he hangs out with those people. I wondered if they'd help their parents in some way at home,´ commented Tariq.

"The memories floated back to Amir ten years before when Limbung in this same place had blocked his way. His mother had told him to secure salt from Aling Takya when Limbung snatched the bag from his hand and poured the whole contents on the ground, with his friends sniggering at the background calling him names, pushing him where he fell on the muddy ground. He fought back but this gave him a big black eye that he could never forget of his bullying."

`Remember when we had a fist fight, Tariq? I was smaller then, but now he could hardly look at me straight in the eye . . . he seemed to have grown smaller over the years.´

`Time has made the difference, my friend,´ said Tariq.

"To ignore them was the only way to keep away from conflict, so they thought it wise to go the other way. Soon after, they reached the river bank and followed the flow of the water, stepping on rocks to avoid the sticky mud. At this time of the day womenfolk squatted at the river banks to take advantage of the sun to do the washing. Girls enjoy swimming. My sisters and I were quick to see them coming from afar. When we heard their squelching and stomping, we stopped what we were doing and greeted both of them a pleasant morning."

"We smiled at each other and waved goodbyes. Those were the little things that made my day. After some time they had gone far and we lost sight of them, their talking diminishing into inaudible chortles. He was quite a man, the girls giggled and talked about them."

"Along the sides of the river grew handsomely picturesque flowers of red roses, white carnations, red asters and blue gladiolas that blossomed anywhere in Sandakan's tropical atmosphere? Amir picked one red rose, brought it close to his nose and smelled its sweet fragrance. The girls wished that he would give it to any one of them. I love roses and it would have given me joy if Amir had thought of giving it to me."

"Further down the river, the water was clearer they could see the rocks and schools of fish at the bottom. They waded through, washed their faces and played with it to their heart's delight. Some bluish fish scampered swiftly, sleeted among rocks and crevices as they approached, leaving tiny pools of dust behind. On trees colourful birds chirped while dancing on the branches. Infinite beauty was all over the place."

`Let's jog and waste no more time. We'll see more of them ahead, Tariq,´ Amir hesitated, seeing his friend was still enjoying.

"Tariq jumped out of the water and jogged after Amir, who was already walking away."

`There's so much beauty around I can't stop playing,´ Tariq was sorry for dilly dallying.

`Don't be sorry. Nature fascinates me too. We'll be here tomorrow, the following day, every day,´ he said, looking over his shoulder at Tariq who was following closely.

`We've been here a thousand times, they don't bore me,´ justified Tariq.

`I'm confident the girls would have loved them, too. Up there the water was muddled and murky with all the washing, they could see the beauty at the bottom no more. And they would have enjoyed our company,´ Tariq was quick to point out.

`We can't afford to do that right now, my friend. Some other day perhaps when we had the opportunity, and without the thought of people at home waiting, we could invite them to come. Look at the sky! The clouds are getting thicker it may rain before we get back. Besides, the elders would disapprove of it, unless you're ready to take one seriously. I'm not prepared for it yet, friend,´ Amir waved his hand in front of Tariq in disapproval.

"A tick of a silence ensued then Tariq babbled, shilly-shallying at some secrets he had been keeping for himself. `I have a feeling Hana had a crush on you. I caught her stealing a look at you yesterday when we were at the market. My hunches hit a bull's eye a while ago when I caught her again with the same look on her eyes. She likes you my friend. I swear.´"

"Tariq's words made Amir ponder deeply for a beat of a second. `He could be wrong,´ Amir brushed the insinuations away, but his mind kept telling him, `go for it Amir. Would it matter if it were true?.´ Of course it was heart-warming and his fondness of her had been a long time fascination. If Tariq only knew how he felt."

`I couldn't afford to make it up, my friend,´ stated Tariq with all honesty, `and there's no reason for me to lie about it.´

"Amir turned silent. He was suddenly found dwelling at his friend's unexpected revelation. `Everything he says us is too good to be true, being the Rajah's daughter. What with all the exposures she gets from different visitors the Rajah receives every day from different places, from handsome men who have power, skills and wealth to offer? It is highly unlikely. Tariq could be wrong. On the other hand , why would he unnecessarily play with my feelings if it were untrue?´"

"It was only a few years back, the sky was overcast when the cry was heard over the village. It was a baby girl again. The creature was now in his arms wrapped in cotton blanket. The newborn baby's closed eyes were swollen, her body delicately tender and soft. Rajah Cali gazed at his daughter with awe, admiring how nature made her to become a little pretty human being. In no time she would be running around the house. He hugged her close and kissed her tiny fingers."

`You wanted a boy. Would you still love her in spite of what came out?´ her wife searched his face for an answer, still weak of childbirth.

`Oh, it would make no difference anymore, *ibu*. She's so tender,´ replied the father.

`What would you like to name her?´ she shifted her legs to stretch.

`How about giving her the name of Hana? After having Sampa and Guita, I'm inclined to name her differently. Yeah, why don't we name her Hana - a name which sounds so feminine, short and easy to remember?´

`Oh, you made me so happy, my dear.´

`Looking at the brighter side, we need not expand the house and put in another room. With a boy we would have to build a separate room exclusively for him.´

`That's what I have been dying to tell you all this time. Another baby girl would be a blessing. Talking about the size of this hut, it's comparably small now, but someday I will build you a bigger one for our children, *ibu*.´

"As time goes by, the little creature crawled, learned to say *ibu,* walked, ran and played with her two elder sisters. She learned to play *bico* with pebbles and jumped through a maze of drawn lines on the streets. Her favourite game was `hide and seek´, where she hid herself from her sisters and for her sisters to let her hide for all the time she wanted."

"She grew up to be a healthy young girl without any hang-ups whatsoever. They said that when she blushed her cheeks turned into pink rosebuds."

"I had grown knowing that I was differently prettier than any other girls in the village. Even my two elder sisters would tell me so. This knowledge never changed anything in me. As I grew up to be a young lady, I noticed young men starting to look at me more often than to any of my two elder sisters who were likewise pretty."

"Rajah Cali, must have been proud of you, Lala," Ilang-ilang beamed with pride.

CHAPTER 4

"The mouth of the river was wide and spacious, extending far out to the sea. In the middle, where the flow of the river ends, a little whirlpool moved endlessly. Everywhere schools of fish of all sizes and kinds competed with the little spaces among themselves as they mouthed and gulped the myriad planktons around. Trout was in every corner. Amir and Tariq went to work right away. They took out their fishing gears and went for the catch, straining their eyes for the bigger ones. They tracked, followed, pierced, gigged and jabbed them skilfully with their spears in calculated movements, wading through waist deep water. Those which they had caught they gathered them at the side of the river. When they figured that they had had enough they jumped out of the water and sat on the green grass to rest."

"The sun was up in the sky they could see their shadows no more, reminding them it was noon time. Their stomachs grumbled, they decided it was time to fill them up. Then they made fire and prepared lunch with the fish they had caught. After cutting the first trout, Tariq started with the second. With a sharp knife he scraped the scales off, clipped the fins and turned the fish over with the belly facing him. Then starting from the gills he made a fine slit up to the tail.

Amir watched him put his thumb in between the gills and in one stroke pulled the entrails out and threw them aside. He handed them to Amir who put them above the fire to grill. *Amir* took out the two *pusós*, cut them in two´s revealing the white rice inside and handed one to Tariq. Grilled fish and rice for lunch, downed with *tubá*. When they finished eating they laid down on their backs to relax."

"They had the whole day to while away. Time was inconsequential, for them it did not exist. With hands folded at the back of their heads, they both looked at the sky far above to daydream, to imagine what was in store in the future. An eagle flew overhead. They watched its graceful passage, its wings extended wide enough to cover the sky as it passed, and Amir wished, that somewhere in time, his dreams of travelling would finally come true. He was ambitious. His life in Sandakan was simple. He could survive by hunting and fishing. But he thought that all he had in Sandakan was not enough. Life was something else beyond the high seas, in one of those faraway places."

`I wonder what we could find in those islands. Are there people like me and Tariq? Do they go fishing and hunting, too,´ he was seeking for an answer. `Someday I would bring Hana with me to see the place, together alone. I wish Tariq's words were true. I love her smile and I love how she looks at me. There's nothing more fulfilling in this life than to have her close, to reach for her any time I want to touch her, or just merely to see her beside me, and to feel her very soul and presence. I'm now more than certain of my feelings . . . then later, raise a family and have children- perhaps plenty of children and without the scrutinizing eyes of the elders,´ a thought flashed across his mind.

"Then they were awakened by the unpredictable weather. Dark clouds were now gathering slowly from the once clear sky, threatening to drop into rain. The sun cowered behind these clouds and the once warm air turned gradually cooler. Then tiny drops of misty rain woke them up, pitter-pattering, giving them hints to get moving, and their reveries went flop in thin air. It was beginning to drizzle. They pulled themselves up and gathered their gears with reluctance."

"Tariq meticulously selected two branches from a tree, cut them off expertly, cleared them with leaves and sharpened one end without further delay. One by one they deftly hitched all the fish together and heaved them onto their shoulders."

`We need some boar's meat at home but I don't think we could still go for the hunt, Tariq,´ calculated Amir, looking at the sky.

`Then we go some other day.´

"Anyway, it was only a week before when boars had been easy preys and they brought home two. The air was heavy and humid. In the stillness, Tariq sneaked behind a snorting boar which was feeding in the woods. When the animal sensed their presence, it darted rapidly through the thicket to hide itself, but Tariq's speed made it impossible for the poor thing to escape the swishing arrow which was right on target. Tariq never missed a shot. Amir who was at his side watched his movements in demobilizing the animal with total admiration."

"Boars were extremely dangerous animals when cornered. They have sharp tusks which could pierce through your skin. One time Tariq was caught surprised by one which was hiding behind him. It charged headlong towards him. If it were not for his friend's quick response, he would have been injured badly."

"Bucks and does were common preys, also mares. But Amir and Tariq preferred to hunt boars. They were plenty in the forest of Sandakan and their meat was tastier."

CHAPTER 5

"It was raining hard when they reached the centre of the village. They took the main road which was eerily deserted. The rooftops dripped, forming pools of water on the ground where the rainwater fell intermittently, the open canals swelled its colour brown with mud. Aling Takya's store at the corner was already closed. Nobody was moving there now. Limbung and the rest had gone somewhere else. One yelping dog crossed to the other side and vanished from sight as soon as they came nearer. The folks they saw in the morning were already gone. Mang Andoy perhaps had already closed its negotiation with his tubá, and probably be back in the security of his hut. The cleaned yards were covered with fallen *lumboy* leaves again. There were no more children playing on the road. In the comfort of their homes, they were tucked inside waiting for food to come on the table with parents who felt secured of their presence. Sunlight which was once so abundant and bright, showering lights on the mountains and the fields on the horizon, now suddenly turned dim and weak."

"Amir's mother waited patiently at the table with the flickering lamp as her company, preparing supper. At the kitchen, the sound of boiling and brewing of salted pork was heard over scorching firewood. On her roof above, the tapping of rain water continued incessantly. It's getting dark and raining, it was unusual for them to be still out in the woods, she was worried, uneasy and anxious of his whereabouts. She remembered him coming home late once, but it was reasonably explained later. Below, at the coop, the chickens were as uneasy as her, clucking wildly."

"They finally got home, Tariq first then Amir striding home alone. Walking on the isolated road he wondered at the tranquility of the familiar place he was passing by. He had an odd sensation that something out of the ordinary might soon happen, some ominous event that he won't ever forget for a lifetime."

"When he reached home he took the stairs then stepped indoors shaking the rain water off his long hair, dumped his hunting equipment and fishing gig then kissed his mother on the cheek.

`What took you so long, son?´ asked his mother who was setting the table for supper, now relieved to see him home."

`This rain made hunting difficult, *ibu*. Boars were nowhere to be found, they seemed to be hiding in some places. I believe they have a natural sense of predicting imminent storms on the way. We've decided to do it some other day. First I dropped Tariq home. We split the catch in half, which in my calculation would last us for two days. It's the wind I was worried we had to call it off.´

"He slumped himself onto a stool tired and weary and stayed there for a while to breathe for a second. From where he was seated he heard the hissing sound of a single wind which found itself inside. He got up and painstakingly followed it by using his face to trace the wind coming inside. When he finally found it he wasted no time to patch it up with a coco husk he had cut into small sizes with his bolo."

"He was confident his hut could still withstand the wind even if it got stronger. His father used to tell him how he drove timbers deep into the ground to make the stilts strong enough to stand any wind. Back in his mind some doubts and apprehensions started building up as to his father's calculations when he heard other hissings again. He had left him early and he considered it as a deception. If he had deceived him, would it also be possible that he would also deceive him about this construction, telling him bed time stories?"

CHAPTER 6

"Talking of bed time stories, one flashed vividly in his mind. It was about his great grandpa, Kusgan and his well-known conquests."

'He had *anting-anting*, which made him stronger than a bull- an amulet which everybody believed had given him this incredible strength and power. In all tribal wars he was leading, killing hundreds with his bare hands, throwing all his enemies easily as if they were light as feather. Great grandpa Kusgan was my hero,' *ayah*'s eyes widened as he recounted the story.

'His powers enchanted me. This made me search for the source of this power. A quest which had led me to pursue it with vigor and zest, leading me to cross the sea to that island which we could see from here,' *ayah* continued.

"*Ayah* was also full of surprises to home-in his stories. Out from his safe, in one of the bamboo post, he took out one of those golden pearls from his velvet bag."

'Look at this,' said his father.

'What is that *ayah*?'

"`It's a pearl.´ He was rolling it in-between his two fingers and raised it above his head. It glowed above the light of the lamp."

`It's beautiful.´

`Yes, it is. And it has magical powers.´

"Then he put it on his palm and closed it into a fist."

`To make one strong!´

"`How?´ Amir's eyes were pinned to his *ayah* innocently."

"`It came from the deep sea. Imagine how it grew to become a pearl inside a shell - over years. Some stayed inside their shells for thousands of years. There's magic in its growing into one like this for years, my son.´ *Ayah*'s eyes widened."

`Your grandpa Kusgan obtained his strength from one of this,´ his father continued.

`Can I use it against Limbung?´

"His father only smiled at his question."

`Not now . . . when you grow up.´

"`How did it give him the power?´ he eyed his *ayah* incredulously."

"`Well, your grandpa Kusgan made a slit on his wrist with a knife and inserted one into it. It was painful and gory but he was so brave. Months passed by for it to heal, of course. When the wound was completely covered one could see the golden pearl embedded through his skin. This made him extraordinarily strong,' *ayah* flexed his biceps to make himself more convincing."

`Why don't you have it in your wrist *ayah,* if it could make you strong?' asked the curious Amir who caught him again this time.

"That was the end of his *anting-anting* story, but the rest about golden horses and flying serpents never failed to arouse his imagination. He was a good father in the real sense of the word. He used to take Amir to hunt with him, taught him how to use the bow and arrow and to shoot perfectly well. They had real time together as son and father and as friends. That was the reason he missed him so much. He missed everything in him."

"Another story, yet the frail young mind clung tightly to it, his total acceptance turned into something that would put a mark as an indelible part of his life in the future. A mark that would propel him to great heights and carve his destiny to become the most landed individual in the history of Sandakan, with properties extending towards the other islands in the north."

"Hmm . . . I love that story, Lala," Ilang-ilang's interest was kindled. Her Lala Hana moved sideways to make herself comfortable, then continued.

CHAPTER 7

"The hurricane came from the northern ocean circling counter clockwise. It started slowly, picked up speed when it entered land and lambasted everything on its way. The howling and hissing got stronger and louder every minute outside, it sounded like a cacophony of musical instruments played out of tune at the same time, rising slowly to staccato. It wiggled its way to find anything to topple down, trees and huts which used to be standing along the river banks. Amir patched up some more hissings he found on the walls. The roof was whipping, it worried him so much. The rhythm was deafening with the banging of a window shutter against the wall somewhere. He could hear leaves and branches rustling and threshing as they sway to and fro. The sound rose to a crescendo, followed by the cracking of branches that got twisted and pulled out from their trunks and the smashing and thudding of trees as they fell on the ground. Smaller trees and plants made snapping sounds as they were uprooted and their hut seemed to vibrate under the force of the winds. The weather now was getting to be violent. The rain continued coming down in roaring torrents. Thunder rumbled and lightning flashed."

"All this chaos made animals go berserk and ran wild about in their coops. Those in the forest were in worst situations, crouching, hiding and searching madly for places to save themselves. Those who were not swift enough to escape the onslaught had found themselves trapped. Birds and monkeys on trees were blown away together with the branches they were holding on to."

"It was dangerous to be outside, there were flying objects that became deadly they cut flesh like sharp knives. In spite of all the dangers, Amir and some men rushed outside and braved the winds to secure their homes. Using strong rattan ropes Amir harnessed moving parts firmly to permanent structures, his stilts held fast. However some roofs gave way and were ripped off, including his. The wind never let up, it became even stronger every minute, and he believed they were in the middle of the eye of the hurricane."

"One flying splinter of wood hit him on the leg. It bled but it didn't hurt him so much. Another hit him at the back, but he struggled to finish what he had to do. He believed his amulet could help him go through it all."

"`Ibu, hold your grip. I'll be in a jiffy to fasten the roof tightly so that it won't go,´ in the middle of all the roaring noise, he climbed up the roof yelling."

"Amir's mother prayed hard to all the *Ginoos* and held on to her most precious possessions. The other men did likewise, which must have been their only recourse. Nevertheless the relentless fury of the wind battered everything that blocked its way without compassion. By the time he was on the ground, he heard a faint sound for help."

`Help!´ the shout became audible now, in the middle of the roaring.

"Amir stretched his hearing, concentrating and tracing where it came from. He looked round. He finally spotted it from a girl who was clinging on to a piece of wood and was carried by the water downstream. He moved hurriedly and followed her, running along the side of the river to learn it was Lara."

"Lara was my childhood friend. She lived nearly beside our home and we played together with my sisters. Her hut was a total wreck and was carried downstream together with all members of her family."

"`Hang on, Lara´ Amir shouted at her who was bobbing in and out of the water. He moved quickly and got a long bamboo pole tucked it under his armpit, ran along the bank as fast as he could far ahead of her and waited. He clung himself with his left arm on a protruding root from a tree to get a steady bearing, waited for her to come to his line, stuck the bamboo pole out for her to hold on to, then with all his remaining strength swung it towards the side of the river. He was amazed at how his strength doubled at the sound of distress, as if he was propelled by an extra-ordinary power from within."

"`Hold still,´ he bellowed. Lara held on until she got closer and closer to the side of the river. Then with all her might crawled frantically, clawing with her fingers onto the muddy bank to safety."

`Are you alright?´ checked Amir.

"Exhausted, Lara only nodded her head. Out of breath and soggy she looked desperately towards her hut which was gliding over the water, unable to express her incapacity to save the rest of her family, her parents and younger brother, who were carried downstream inside."

"`Wait for me here. I hope there's time for me to catch them,´ Amir told her, his vision tracing the mangled hut being carried away by the rushing water. He ran as fast as he could, slipped, stood up, slipped again, regained his balance but they were already far ahead of him and the water was too fast to outrun. He realized his strength wasn't as strong as he thought it to be. He was as human as everybody else."

"The river rose swiftly. It overflowed, spilling over the river banks, flooding lower grounds, the road and farmlands. Several huts along the banks were torn into pieces or carried whole downstream, together with their occupants. It was horrifying to hear them shout for help as heads bobbed above the water for air and then went under again, never to come up anymore. Amir was desperate to help but he could do nothing to save them in the dark, much more when he heard them call `help! Help!´ his heart sank helplessly."

"The hurricane's four hour violent whirling attack on the village had left so many people homeless and desperate from lost love ones. Standing structures were violently uprooted. Those stronger ones had been broken into two and blown away."

"Never had he ever witnessed such a brutal carnage and devastating as this one in Sandakan in his entire lifetime. There were occasional storms and typhoons but this one was so ferocious it seemed the *Ginoos* were angry with the village. `Oh, God, why God,´ Amir called out to heaven."

"On the other side of the river Tariq's hut held on. The hurricane's dreadful drama brought devastation beyond description on the other parts. It spared nothing except Tariq's hut which was well covered by the mountain and far from the epicentre. His mother thought it was a miracle their hut stood still."

"`Are all the animals safe?´ inquired Tariq."

"`They are all in the coop except the ox, but I transferred it near the acacia tree when it started to rain. They're all safe in there.´ Eman roared in the middle of the raging storm."

"`It was the smartest move you've done, Eman ,´ Hakim shouted back."

`I'll go down and check again.´

`Be careful,´ cautioned Hakim.

CHAPTER 8

"The sky opened up and moonbeams filtered through thin clouds, which spread light into the valley again. The wind subsided and finally dropped away. Its passage was as quick as how intense it had been. From howling the sound now fettered into the hissing of the tail wind."

"What followed was awkward stillness, interspersed with the croaking of the frogs, chirping of crickets and the trickles of water everywhere. Survivors poured out one by one in trepidation, still awestruck at the horrendous magnitude of the hurricane. The rain abated a bit, and little showers continued to fall. The deafening sound turned into the moaning of the wounded and wailings of unlucky ones who lost properties and loved ones."

"The raging river receded slowly, now rolling with mud and debris downstream to find its way into the sea."

"Amir stood dazed at his doorway, gazing up at the sky looking for some answers. A light breeze brushed his face gently, he felt oddly uncomfortable despite its coolness. The night was dark but he could still make out familiar shapes afar: the bridge, piles of timber woods, a lone coco tree still standing gawkily, the *lumboy* tree cut into half, and Tariq's hut at the other side of the river."

"A pang of hunger suddenly came, so he got back inside and asked his *ibu* for food, dropped on a stool and looking up he saw the hollowed space where his roof used to be standing, now ripped off from its usual place. He glanced at his mother with compassion, and then sighed that reached as far as the moon."

"He finished his meal in thoughtful solitude, numbed of the effect the hurricane had brought them. The rain had definitely stopped but still he heard drippings of water everywhere."

"He took a deep breath then sought permission to see Tariq. Before slipping out, he gave his mother a kiss on the cheek. On his way he saw the scope of destruction: splinters and pieces of wood all over in heaps mixed with mangled nipas and shredded coco leaves once used to be part of their homes. His heart sank to see friends scourging debris, searching for lost loved ones, calling out their names in desperation. Disorder and confusion was beyond description. All of this, but his mind was on somebody. Where could she be, he searched himself for an answer. He looked around to see only familiar faces. In darkness he could still make out who they were but not a trace of her."

"Rajah Cali would have called an emergency meeting if he were around. Everybody wondered where he was. Amir wondered too. Most people regarded him as an affectionate leader and tonight everybody was expecting him to be at their side at this time of crisis. Was he a casualty?"

"Far away in another village Rajah Cali could not contain himself from worrying."

"We had a grand time celebrating but his mind was back in Sandakan. We had to cut our stay and went back to see what became of our home. We packed up and started for the road back in the middle of the night. He figured that before dawn we would have reached the village, never expecting that what we would see were rubbles and debris all over."

"When we entered Sandakan what welcomed my vision was beyond my imagination. Wreckage was everywhere where the huts along the river used to be standing and survivors were gauntly moving around to retrieve lost possessions and loved ones. Broken trees and fallen structures were blocking the roads making our entrance difficult and slower. We edged forward to be met by haggard and desperate faces who were eager to tell their stories. It was moving and heartbreaking. Much more when we found out our house was already among the rubbles and debris, flattened and uninhabitable."

"It was already dawn when Amir left Tariq behind after a long talk. He was glad his friend suffered only minor damages. He had a large hut by local standard which had been built by his father. The back frame was practically pegged onto the side of the mountain dredged purposely vertically up to the top, which made it sturdier against strong winds, winds that often come during the monsoon season."

"On his way back home, he was amazed at how the beam bridge had survived among the ruins still hanging intact over the now tranquil waters. Beyond the horizon the skyline showed an eerie look. On crossing back to his side he saw people retrieving bodies from the river. He was wondering if these people would ever know how many had drowned or drifted downstream. He felt considerably lucky to have been among those who survived and guilty at the same time for not having the strength to accept the destiny that had befallen on his people."

"As daylight shone brightly over the whole village Amir wondered if it could recover easily. Relief activities were being conducted at the clearing in the market. On ordinary days it had been the hub of traders and buyers: Women tugged baskets, haggled and bargained and shop attendants shouted at assistants to replenish stalls, which became half empty of green fresh vegetables and fruits. Even children used to play at the clearing. Today it had been converted into an emergency centre, where the wounded lay waiting for medical attendance. Survivors who lost their homes hunched at the corners wondering where they could stay for the night."

"Food was also distributed by those who had extra to share. Rajah Cali and his family were among those who took care of the people. He was distributing rice and salt fish. Amir was relieved to see that the Rajah was at the helm of all the activities. For him it meant I was there, too, and it took him not so long to spot me attending to some children and the wounded and his heart sighed with relief."

"Amir's impulse told himself to come nearer. When I saw him, my heart leapt with joy, relieved to see somebody to relate with and share the sufferings and the bursting pain within. I wanted also to be near him."

"`How are you Amir,´ was all I could muster to speak, my eyes glowed with tears. I wanted to cry on his shoulder, to tell him how it all broke my heart."

"`I have been looking for you,´ he said. There was a genuine tone of concern on his voice. I was waiting for him to say something heart-warming like saying he missed me. Instead he told me about the hurricane, how strong it was, the deafening sounds, the drowning of people at the river and all the grief he saw afterwards. Then he asked politely where I had been."

"I told him I was at the next village when the hurricane hit, regretful that I had not been there with them and would have more than willing to share the sufferings and losses when our people where fighting with the winds. In that fleeting of a second we were bonded together, tacit but deep, our hands touched, our eyes met but it was a different bonding. It was the bonding of two suffering hearts who had shared a common painful experience."

"`So, that was the reason why the Rajah was nowhere to be found,´ Amir thought."

"At midday before it struck, our entire family and all household members had gone to a nearby village, invited to a formal lunch celebration which was my uncle's daughter's wedding, my cousin. Looking at it in a different light the invitation was a saving grace. We would have also suffered the hurricane's devastating power. Who would ever know that one of us in the household would have also suffered the same fate as the rest who went down the river? My uncle's village was far from the epicentre, we only felt light winds. When we came back to Sandakan we found out our home was already among the wreckage."

"`There's no way that Rajah Cali would run from responsibility,´ Amir was more relieved to learn this."

CHAPTER 9

"In no time Amir's lost roof was replaced with Tariq's help. They stitched the coconut leaves together, put up the bamboo structures, cutting them here and there, and sewing them together to form the plies."

"`Sandakan brings so much bad memories Tariq. I think time has come for a change. Those mountains . . . remember them? They are calling me to go. *Baguio* had taken all our friends away. What if he comes again?´ asked Amir, wondering."

"`That's wistful thinking, my friend. Think it over. We've been in Sandakan for as long as I can remember. Supposing life's worse in those mountains?´ replied Tariq after moving over to the next ply of coconut roofing."

`We would lose nothing except perhaps . . . our efforts. I feel there's something for us there where we could settle and claim lands. God willing we could come back when we see life. Nothing taken, nothing gained. A change is a soothing balm from the disaster.´

"`Do you remember what the elders used say: be wherever you are, to be yourself and harness all the resources within your means, with all strength and power to follow your dreams,´ said Tariq."

`Yes, I do. They also say that it would be easier to catch fish in a river where there's plenty and easier still to hunt in a forest where there's plenty of games to hunt, I'm confident out there the idea of plenty is immeasurable.´

`Wake up, friend. How do you think you'd take us to those mountains? Tell me.´

`It's clear in my mind we could think of some ways. If I could only fly I would have been there already. If I were a fish I could slitter into the sea and would have been there long time before. I'd do it whatever it takes. And I dread the thought that some of our brothers are now resting side by side with the fish we are eating.´

"`That thought has given me some trouble, too,´ Tariq concurred smiling at his friend's comment."

`I remembered how my father built a certain kind of raft from bamboos stitched together with rattan strips. I estimated in sixty sun risings, when the moon comes to full face, it would have been finished, if we started soon. I have no doubt about it, my heart tells me so, my friend.´

`My heart is still not on it yet. Show me the way then I'll follow. And would your heart be at rest if some lions devoured your Hana in our absence?´

Amir changed the subject, "I'm pretty glad your family survived the onslaught, Tariq. Honestly, I wish I knew how you did it."

"`My friend, everything was in the hands of the *Ginoos*. We prayed hard without stopping until it stopped. My tongue can't tell you exactly how our hut stood firm. I believe it was providence's will for me to see the day. Do you not wonder how your Hana came out of it? I know and I would tell you if you want me to,´ Tariq responded, as a matter of fact, before going down from the roof."

"`I saw her at the market this morning with her family. We had a short talk, Tariq. They arrived from a cousin's wedding celebration; she looked so pretty in her new dress. I think she was out of place among the desolation. Poor Hana, I saw her so tired and sleepy. Their home was also destroyed and they don't have any place to stay for the night. And remember, if we're going I won't leave any stones unturned until she knows how I feel for her,´ declared Amir as he was following his friend down the ladder."

"On hearing Amir's revelation, Tariq's ears stood up unbelieving, agape at the spontaneity of his statement. He knew him so well, but had been unable to fathom into the inner sanctum of his feelings as yet, for being so conservative and secretive about them. His insinuations before had not given up to open his heart. Now he's surprised to hear his friend finally pouring out his true feelings for her."

CHAPTER 10

"It took some days to return to normal times, to forget, longer. Thanks to the invaluable aid coming from other neighbouring villages, Sandakan was able to cope up with the disaster: medicine and food arrived from the other villages in droves; potable water was restored and the market came back to normal activity, where necessary commodities could be seen in stalls again; new houses started rising. Hakim was beginning to be busy constructing them. For the meantime the Rajah and his family had a temporary makeshift home while the building of a permanent one was going on."

`How long would it take you to finish it, Hakim?´

`I can't tell you the number of days it would take me, Rajah, but I would continue to labour until you have the rooms to live in. If my two brothers decided to help me, then it would be ready in no time.´

"`First I want to know the number of rooms you planned it to be divided,´ stated Hakim."

`There should be at least five bedrooms in it, two kitchens, a large reception room or salon, an *ibuh rumah* and two outhouses. I had envisioned the *ibuh rumah* to be comfortable. Remember . . . that's where we would be spending most of our time.´

`There's one more thing, Rajah. I'll request Eman to draw me out a plan for your house, and talk with him if he could devise something to make it easy to clean the outhouses. He's been thinking of a way to do away with fetching water from the well. So far he has come up nothing with the mechanics yet.´

`I trust you could do it, Hakim.´

`Thank you, Rajah Cali,´ he said and left.

"It took four seasons for the brothers to finish Rajah Cali's house. Everyone in the village agreed that it had been a marvellous model in house construction. With five bedrooms on the second floor and two more downstairs, it was so spacious worthy of being the house of a Rajah. Colourful flowers abound in the garden in front as you enter the gate, then you go up to a large salon with wooden floors made of *dau*. This was their *ibuh rumah*. Most carpenters love *dau* due to its strength and durability, but some hated it because it was harder than their cutting tools. They said it was so hard their tools had to be sharpened or changed every now and then continually."

"Rajah Cali still insisted they use coconut materials for the roof. They bring coolness in warm weather, he said. Tiles and bricks were of little use because they absorb heat instead of reflecting them, so they were preferred less in warm climate."

"We three sisters had a room for each one on the second floor. My room was the envy to both of my sisters who considered it to be well situated, facing the morning sun. Overlooking the window, I had a good view of the garden below and the mountains far beyond. Fresh air was abundant coming from the forest. Except during rainy days, the windows were always open to let the forest air come in and out to cool the rooms in warm afternoons."

"Hakim built two kitchens. One for display and the other was the real kitchen. The real one which they always called the dirty kitchen was built separately from the main building where the kitchen personnel cook food and for the family to take their meals every day. Some people questioned the logic of what he had built. Not only after several use and seeing the black soot on the walls and ceiling that they appreciated the logic of the construction."

`There's one problem to my construction, my dear brother,´ he confided.

"`I know what it is. Cleaning and washing? It always had been and always will be,´ said Eman ."

`Yes, it's a large house and the housekeepers had to fetch water from far away. What I want is for them to be unnecessarily burdened, with abundant water to clean the house without the need and extra effort of going to the spring. The Rajah requested if I could devise something that could unburden the women and the girls in going to the spring or river every time they wash clothes and take a bath- something that could let them do these at the comfort of their home. Can you think of something?´

`Let me see.´ Eman was pensive.

`Something not too complicated.´

`What I'm thinking is one which might replace the job of the water supplier. Poor guy he would be out of job.´

`I know you could devise something.´

`Yes, I think I have something in my mind. Just give me enough time to work out the mechanics. What if we build a canal from the spring to his hut?´

`The water could easily be contaminated. That would be messy, unless the canal is closed with something, more or less permanently.´

`It had to be a close conduit unexposed to the dust, animals and insects that could contaminate the water. The only material I could think as of now is the bamboo. It's long and easy to acquire.´

`Remember there are nodes you have to deal with.´

`These can be taken out one by one with a long sharp pointed object.´

'Ok, I trust your judgment on this, brother. I'd leave it all up to you.'

'So it would be bamboos then.'

CHAPTER 11

"Days and months rolled, seasons changed. Years turned around as time fleeted by. Recovery was in the air: farmers made abundant harvest; trade flourished and new homes went up everywhere. Rajah Cali's house was finished and stood as one example of Hakim's architectural genius. Life returned to normal times."

"However poor Amir made no progress with his intentions as yet. I had been waiting for him to declare his feelings. He was stalling for the right time. Whatever his reasons maybe he only knew, and the longer he waited the more he was falling afar and suffering. The longer I waited the more I was falling in love with him. What kept him from holding was a real puzzle to me and to his friends."

"Tariq fitted another arrow and released it. Hakim and Eman applauded approvingly when they saw that he hit the target, bull's eye for the third time."

"`Perfect shot,´ commented Amir on time to see it, incredulously shaking his head at the skill of Tariq."

`Practice builds great shots, my friend. I do it all the time because I love doing it. Did you hear about Lara?´ asked Tariq.

`What about her?´

"`I heard she was engaged, getting married. People say the guy was lucky. She's also lucky because now she has somebody to share her life with. The same people were also asking if you were as lucky in your pursuit with Hana. If you'd tell her, we could have a double wedding!!´ he continued talking, and then fitted another arrow. He released it and made a bull's eye again."

`Nah, I have my reservations. Time will come that I would have to come out from my shell and tell her,´ Amir said this, looking away.

"`When is the time, my friend? You have been focused the other way,´ stated Tariq more persuasively."

"The challenge from his friend struck him right into the core of his being. Amir turned to himself in contemplation, `Tariq is right. My mind has been focused on my ambition, in such a way that I have been setting aside other equally important things in my life. I have been putting off Hana and making false excuses to justify my cowardice. There must be a way for her to know, he thought. Ask her hand from the Rajah was an alternative, a good alternative in fact. So be it and it should be right now or never.´"

"`Right now,´ he said boldly. Tariq tipped his head a little, with a smile, upon hearing his statement, dubious at his boldness this time."

"He bid goodbye to his friends, and left them with a resolved mind. Right now was the time. He brushed his hair up with his fingers and dashed for the road in the direction of the Rajah's home mustering all the courage he had. He rehearsed his line, word for word, in his mind, repeating several times to commit them to memory. When he was at the door he stopped and hesitated, thinking of what the Rajah would say. He still had time to pull it off. Would he react differently? Then he decided to go for it and knocked on the door. He passed his fingers through his hair again, mustering all the courage, waiting for it to open."

"Our young maid opened the door."
`Yes?´
`Is the Rajah free? Can you tell him Amir's here to talk with him, please?´
"`A moment ,please,´ the maid told him to wait, and closed the door behind her. In a few minutes, it opened again and the same girl told him to come in."

`The Rajah is waiting for you at the salon, Amir. Please come in.´

"Amir stepped inside, nervous and in awe at the spaciousness of the hall and the luxury of everything in it. Hakim had made an exceptionally good work for the Rajah, he thought. A sudden strange feeling of inferiority bordering on not coming up with expectations came upon him. He looked at his bare feet and felt they were no match to the shiny *dau* wood floor he was treading on. Moving on, his eyes relished at the sight of the ornaments on the wall. He saw a shield crisscrossed with two long spears on the wall on his right. On the left was a two meter bow with a quiver full of arrows beside it. His walk turned awkward, he almost fell out of balance. As he approached the Rajah smiled at him."

`Come near, Amir. Have a seat.´

`Thank you Rajah.´

`Before anything, would you like to have some tea?´

Amir nodded courteously. `That would be fine.´

"The servant girl left after Rajah Cali made a sign for her to bring them green tea. Then he started to pose for an answer, as a matter of course."

`What brings you here?´
`It is a matter which is personal to me, Rajah Cali, to come and seek your permission.´
`Hmm . . . It must be of some importance?´
`Yes, indeed.´
`Have you seen how the people have been able to deal with the devastation, now they're building their homes again?´
`Yes, Rajah, I'm glad they have.´

`I'm exceedingly thankful to Hakim and his brothers for this house. Haven't you seen how he labored for it?´

`It is indeed magnificent, Rajah!´

"An interruption ensued when the same servant girl brought their teas and laid them on the table, close enough for them to reach. Rajah Cali took one cup for him and signaled Amir to take one for him."

`What is it, Amir?´

"`I have wanted to tell you,´ he paused in the middle of his sentence, feeling a lump of air blocking his throat, then he sipped his tea to clear the air."

"`Tell me, my son. What is it in your mind,´ the Rajah prompted him, sipping his tea."

`Your permission is what I'm here for, Rajah.´

"Instead of replying immediately, he looked at the ornaments on the walls, trying to find the right words to say, the ones he had memorized were gone."

"`What about? If it's within my means,´ Rajah Cali was patient and encouraged him more, . . . get to the point.´"

"He opened his mouth halfway and closed it again. He looked at his feet. In spite of all the prodding he couldn't take his courage out. He shyly looked at the Rajah, summing up all his remaining courage in trepidation. He was about to say what he came for, but his mind would not let him, drying his throat, making his heart thud desperately, filling him with a sickening feeling of dread that was unexplainable. He was afraid of rejection or ridicule, which prevented him from saying what was actually in his heart."

`I want to . . . chop trees from the forest . . .´

"`What a jerk I am,´ he disparaged himself silently."

`I thought it proper to talk with you first before doing it.´

`Mmm . . . And what're you going to do with them?´

`It's been my dream of going places, beyond the great seas, Rajah. And today I've decided to do it . . . to follow that dream . . . I will build a boat,´ pointed out Amir after recovering himself.

`Do you know how you would go about it? I haven't heard of anybody who has done something like this as yet.´

"He looked at him admiringly."

`I would need the help of Hakim on this. Eman and Tariq would also help in the construction.´

"`How many trees do you need?´ Rajah Cali was sizing him up."

`Five to ten, perhaps.´

`Hmm . . . I want your assurance that any wastage on the trees should be avoided.´

`I assure you of my best intentions on this Rajah Cali.´

`So then, you have my unconditional approval, Amir. When are you starting?´

`Immediately, Rajah.´

`Do you need any help?´

`Well, I have the best team in town.´

"When he went to leave, he had some misgivings to himself, rueful in a certain way. He had let the opportunity slip in his hands. `Why was it difficult to tell anybody when it's about my feelings,´ he asked himself, making some assessments as to the reasons for his cowardice. `I think this is the reason some men can't get a girl of their own, their feelings hidden in the shyness of their characters. If *ayah* was here he could have helped me to raise my intentions to the Rajah. I don't have a father to do it anymore. If I had to seek the hands of Hana for marriage, I would have to do it alone by myself.´"

CHAPTER 12

"After his conversation with the Rajah, Amir went straight to Tariq to talk and to pour out his frustrations to himself. He knew his friend could make him feel better. On the other hand, he could also confirm with Hakim if he had the time to help him in the boat project."

`I know you have the tools your father left you and your experience in construction. I'm confident you could do it for me,´ he said, looking at Hakim.

`I can assure you nothing, Amir. I don't know how, in the first place. Besides, I have a lot of projects going on right now,´ Hakim said.

`Let's see if we could use Eman here for ideas.´

`Tariq, I remembered you had an axe your father left you. It'd come in handy when we go to the forest tomorrow. We´ll cut enough of the best woods then bring them all down to the riverside,´ reminded Amir of his friend.

`No problem. I would have it ready tonight.´

`And could you Eman bring your ox with you?´

"Eman nodded to signify his acceptance."

`I'm confident we could do it. We have Hakim and Eman here to help us, Tariq. With all the resources and the brains we have, I would have no doubts about it.´

Tariq cut the flow of conversation to inquire, `Amir, how's your conversation with the Rajah?´

`I couldn't tell him my friend . . . I was a jerk,´ he replied , looking at the ground.

"`My friend, It's difficult to understand what you missed . . . you had it all within your reach. Why did you hold it from the Rajah,´ inquired Tariq, shaking his head disbelieving."

"`I was speechless, Tariq. My courage left me when I saw the majesty of the place. I was a complete fool, I underestimated myself, I considered she would be good for a prince,´ Amir confessed."

`So it was all about your inferiority. Don't you see that you are far better than any guys here in Sandakan? Well, there will always be opportunities. Next time, you should be brave, my friend. Tell him straight in the eye, without any fear and second thoughts. Remember there are a couple of men who are interested in her, too. It may be too late for you next time. Or there will be no other time.´

"`For the present time we would have to concentrate on how we would do about the boat construction or whatever it is that could take us out into the sea. I sought the Rajah's permission for us to cut some trees ,´Amir concluded."

"It took them the whole night to talk about the project. They argued and fought with ideas. As soon as Hakim laid the plan, the brother's excitement rose to great heights. To secure the materials was the next move."

CHAPTER 13

"A new dawn broke, the air was invitingly cool, and totally uplifting. Roosters crowed as always. Village folks did their usual chores, and Amir strutted his way to the forest beside Tariq and Hakim. Eman was tugging his ox behind."

"The forest occupied a large patch of land that spanned from the plains to the mountains. It's a thick green patch where *balete, dau, nara, acacia* and all kinds of tropical trees grew. The recent hurricane did little to destroy most of its centuries old trees which they needed for the boat construction."

"The team started choosing the trees they would have to cut down marking them with colours. They worked fast and soon cut down enough trees; they trimmed off leaves and branches then rolled the logs over to be fastened together in one bundle. Eman yoked the ox then fastened the bundle behind it. When they were ready, off they went marching down to the river dragging the logs behind."

"Hakim had been thinking of the construction since Amir made the proposal to him. This was his first boat and started without any ideas as to its form or looks. He had mulled the new challenge over and over, measuring all angles and considerations to weigh with utmost precision such as the size, balance and durability. Then there was seaworthiness."

"`What if we failed?´ he questioned himself, wavering in his confidence."

"But soon recovered and took charge. `Now, men listen. This is a great task before me, and the first of its kind. I'm convinced we could do it with your cooperation and suggestions as to how we should do it. Your sketch, Eman, is very useful, it has given me some ideas where to start. Let's start by hewing the logs into shape and build Amir's boat,´ pronounced Hakim, now building up his confidence."

`Remember. We measure before we cut. We'll do the process twice all the time. If we do our work this way we save time, effort and materials.´

"Everybody agreed without question at Hakim's logic."

"They started with the hull, which gave them some headaches. They argued if it were to be flat or curved. The geometry was confusing. Finally they decided on a concaved hull. The hull was laborious and longer to work with but they worked it out cheerfully, chiselling, gouging and scooping out the inner parts, until they got the exact form in Eman's sketch. He figured out a way to obtain the aerodynamic effect by shaping the front end. When the body was formed their spirits ran high. Then they followed it up with the ribs which were installed across, and then laid the planks permanently with pegs and joints. For balance, they chose bamboo poles which had been dried first, then installed them as outriggers on both sides. Last were the oars and the moorings. Three full moons and the boat took shape."

"On trial day, they checked if the balance was correct and the boat was water tight. They pushed it unto the river and observed if it tipped to any side. After deciding that it was sea worthy they push it back to the riverbank and made it rest on its rack."

"On the day the finishing touches were applied to the boat, our household was rocked by some terrible event. It worried my father so much; I remembered how he aged in so little time."

CHAPTER 14

"Some members of our household thought I ran away with Amir. It was during supper time when they learned of my absence. Meal time was sacred and everybody was expected to be at the table when food was ready. The housekeeper made the call several times and I was nowhere to come down from my room."

"Rajah Cali summoned all the household members to the salon, who lined up in front of him, waiting for his words. He was pacing back and forth with a look of consternation and worry on his face. Deep lines were evident on his forehead."

`Who knows where Hana is,´ was his first question.

`Did she say anything? Some clues as to where she was going, I don't remember your sister going somewhere without saying anything.´

"No word, even from the most reliable hands in the kitchen."

"He was looking at each and every one of them, searching for clues. They were all quiet, innocent as a petal, obviously clear they knew nothing of my disappearance or whereabouts. My father suspected I ran away with somebody or eloped with a boyfriend."

"`Ayah, she went out to see Lara as she always does,´ Sampa volunteered in a low voice, after seeing that nobody dared to say anything."

"`At about what time Sampa,´ Rajah Cali stopped pacing and faced Sampa."

"` Exactly before supper time, *ayah*. It's definitely true . . . ´ interrupted Guita, your other aunt."

`I want you all to tell me the truth. Have there been any happenings here without me knowing it?´

`No, *ayah*.´

`It wouldn't matter if you had some secrets, as long as she is safe and sound. I want you to tell me if she was seeing somebody or having a rendezvous with someone, a boyfriend, perhaps.´

"`Ayah, Hana told me she was going to Lara's. I went to talk to Lara and she swore Hana left her to have supper. When she sent her off she saw Limbung in front of her house as if waiting for someone,´ stated Guita. Her statement made the Rajah think for a second."

`Guita, I know you are intimately close. Has she mentioned anything to you on a personal level - anything that would suggest something out of the ordinary?´

`Well . . . she tells me everything, *ayah*. We have no secrets. I mean we share all our secrets and what's on our mind. She told me everything, including those intimate ones. She even told me about the guys who were closer to her heart and those who weren't, whom she's fond of and whom she isn't. ´

`Go on,´ prodded Rajah Cali.

`She told me she likes Amir more than anybody else. But she's keeping it to herself because the poor guy has never shown any signs that would tell her so, so far.´

`Mmm . . . Is there anybody else who'd be interested in your sister? ´

`Well, we know nothing about Amir because he has spoken not a single word as yet, but Limbung, yes.´

`Who on earth is this Limbung?´

Then the name came back to Rajah Cali. `Is he the son of Celi Ngan, near the bridge?´

`Yes, *Ayah*, Limbung Ngan.´

"`I see . . .That would be all for now. Go back to what you have been doing. Ondo, tell Limbung I would like to see him . . . now,´ ordered Rajah Cali to one of the boy runners."

"Limbung was the son of a wealthy farmer, Ngan. During the hurricane all their harvest was lost, but now that progress had come back, their living had also improved considerably. I ignored him all the time. I considered his advances as nothing more than aggressiveness borne out of haughtiness. And the more he showed interest, the more I stayed afar."

"In a few minutes Ondo came with Limbung."

"`Come forward, Limbung,´ enjoined Rajah Cali, who watched his movements to see any signs of unusual behaviour."

"'I heard Hana's not home yet, Rajah. I reckoned this is what I came for, to tell you her whereabouts. There's nothing I could tell you,' Limbung's show of disrespect to the Rajah Cali manifested in his delivery and tone of voice, not realizing that his statement gave him away."

`I see . . . Have you seen her today, Limbung?´
`No, I have never,´ he lied.
"This is all what Raja Cali wanted to know. Only one lie that would give him away."

`That would be all, Limbung. You can go and thank you for coming. If you learned of something, do come forward without hesitation.´

"Limbung looked at the sky and estimated he had time. He headed up the river, crossed the bridge and disappeared himself into the forest."

"After Limbung had left, Rajah Cali ordered Ondo, the boy runner, for Amir to come. It didn't take him long to appear from the riverside. He was almost running, the boy following behind."

`Take your seat, Amir. I knew your father so well. He was an honest person, your mother, too. Now, I want you to tell me frankly. Did you see Hana today?´

"Amir hesitated to respond for fear of any repercussions, still catching his breath. He was about to say no but decided he had to be honest."

`Yes, at the market, I think, buying food with Sampa and Guita, and some of her escorts this morning.´

`Did you get to talk to her?´

`I wanted to but there was no way with all the other girls around. I only waved at her and she waved back at me. Why Rajah . . . anything wrong?´

`Hana hasn't been home yet and I want to know where she'd gone. She's a special girl to me, and I want nothing more than her presence. Tell me truthfully, Amir. I feel incapable of soliciting this question but for the sake of my daughter I would have to do it. I want an honest answer from you. Do you happen to have some feelings for my daughter . . . I mean, do you like her?´

"The question shot like lightning, which took Amir by surprise but still he was able to maintain his equanimity. Silence hovered for a moment. He had never anticipated answering as direct a question as this one. He weighed his options carefully. Should he keep silent, take a breath and explain later when he was back to his senses? His mind reeling, he could look at the Rajah straight in the eye no more. This was it. Strike while it's still fresh. This would be the moment I was waiting for, he told himself. If I denied the fact, I would be a fool."

"The Rajah was looking at him, waiting for his answer. Courage came back."

`Yes, Rajah Cali. In fact this is what I've been dying to tell you so much, for so long. I care for her. Remember the last time I came? I wanted to tell you so, but my courage left me. I love your daughter and I'm ready to marry her.´

"The Rajah was not as much as surprised to hear it. If Amir had known the Rajah would react positively to his revelation, he would have already told him the first time he came, without fear and reservations."

`Hmmm . . . It isn't hard to believe you Amir, I trust you. I know you are a good person. I know your family and your late father. But what is first and foremost is to find her. For the time being, I want you to do something for me and this would only be between the two of us. Do you know Limbung? ´

`Yes, Rajah Cali.´

`I want you to watch him closely. Track his movements, what he does and where he goes. Then report back to me. I know little how you're going to do this, but you have my blessings. You may do this alone or with the help of your friends. My primary concern is to bring my daughter back, safe and sound. Go now and be careful.´

"Rajah Cali was the leader of our tribe and a wise one. He ruled our people with compassion and kindness. Being the Rajah his powers were encompassing and without limits. He made laws and execute them. He was also as tough as a stone for those who crossed his ways and as fair and just as any Rajahs in his decisions."

"Contemplating deeply Amir left, going over and over all the conversation he had with Rajah Cali to get some logical explanations. `How on earth did this happen?´ he searched himself. `After the great winds, now this sudden tragedy, a tragedy which most wretchedly had befallen to the one I love most than anything in this world. Where could she be right now?´ he closed his hand into a fist, as the thought struck him. He felt he was in the middle of a difficult conundrum, full of uncertainties and doubts. He had no idea where to start. He had known Limbung, his association with shady characters and his interest. But this was not enough. He might be as innocent as anybody else. He needed hard facts, facts that could pinpoint him to my disappearance."

"`If something happened to her, he would have to answer to me,´ he swore to himself. When he got back to the site, his three friends were still working with the boat excitedly waiting for some good news."

"`How was it, my friend? Tell us,´ Tariq was curious. He put down his tools, took a piece of cloth then wiped them clean from sawdust."

`Bad news . . . It's worse than what you think it is. Hana's gone and nobody knows where she is,´ muttered Amir, downcast.

"`What?´ Eman came closer to listen more intently."
`Did she run with somebody,´ questioned Tariq.

`Nobody knows. That is something I must have to investigate. Rajah Cali told me to do it. He said it was fishy, he smelled foul play. He told me it was unlikely of her to leave without saying anything.´

`No leads at all?´ Hakim inquisitively joined in.

`He suspected Limbung. Lara swore she saw him nearby at the time of her disappearance.´ "Amir put his two hands over his face in desperation."

`I knew it. Smart aleck, eh,´ commented Hakim, who had been silently attentive to the conversation.

`What if there's somebody else behind?´ Tariq wondered.

"`I know his friends who are also questionable, they could be probable suspects,´ responded, Eman, who also put down the tool he's handling to participate in the conversation."

`How can that foolish guy think he could get away with it, here in this small village?´ said Hakim.

`What should I do? I'm helpless,´ confessed Amir honestly looking for support.

`We can't leave you alone on this, Amir. We'll help you. What are friends for,´ consoled Tariq.

`It makes me feel better having friends like you, Tariq. Rajah Cali Insisted that I should report to him, for whatever things may come out.´

`We'll do that as soon as we had something in our hands,´ Tariq said.

`I have a plan and it's simple. Here's what I think we should do: Tonight we'll watch him closely, station ourselves in front of his hut and around it. It's with utmost importance that he suspects nothing or knows nothing of what we are doing. In the darkness we use some of the tricks we used to do. Remember the colors and the sounds we used to play with, Tariq? Now, if nothing would come out of it, then we'll have to think of some other ways. What's important is that we act without delay,´ suggested Eman.

"Then he laid out everything, explaining their moves in detail and instructing each one his respective role, `first we go home and have supper. Then we'll see each other again.´"

"After covering the boat with leaves they parted ways."

CHAPTER 15

"Sandakan was a small village with a simple structure, having no more than one principal road that went along the length of the river, traversed by few unpaved footpaths. If one had to look for something, it would have to be going from one hut to the other to find it. Besides, something like the disappearance of a person could never be hidden for a long time without being discovered in a small place. The logical assumption was that I could be somewhere far from Sandakan. Some sceptics thought I was hiding myself intentionally and did not want my family to know it. But this was far from being logical. Those with common sense thought I was somewhere else outside of the village, kept against my will."

"I had no idea where I was. Immersed in deep thought and looking for reasons as to why this was happening, I shifted my legs to shake off the numbness. Limbung had been a childhood neighbour and the last person I expected to do such a nameless act, much less to tie my two feet and hands and drag me to this place. Jilting him was the reason. But would he do that to a girl whom he loved, if he truly loved her? This was no love at all. I thought of my family and friends who must already be so worried, my father Rajah Cali, my *ibu*, and sisters Sampa and Guita and Amir . Did he know about this? Would he do something for me if he knew how I was feeling at that time, of how lonely and desperate I was? Oh, how I wished he did, but would it matter to him if he knew, I pondered woefully."

"I never stopped worrying and I sobbed. Beyond where I was held captive, small strange sounds made me shudder in fear: the gnawing in the night, the chirping of crickets and the hissing of a snake. I could hear the shuffling of the guards and their murmurings and the occasional snorting of the ox that took us there. The darkness and the eerie sound of the night were distressing."

"They dumped me in a lonely decrepit hut in the middle of the thick forest. It was a secret place and locating it was difficult if not impossible by going straight through thick trees and bushes. The only way was to follow the river upstream along the river bank. About a mile from the village was another hanging bridge that crossed to the other side which would lead to a hidden muddy path entering the dark forest, consisting of a large complex maze of crisscrossing muddy footpaths. Outside were two ruffians seated at the table cleaning their weapons, keeping watch around the hut. Not far away was the white ox tied to a tree munching on leaves used to carry me to that place. I was inside seated on a straw mat on the floor with hands and feet tied with a rope."

"When night engulfed the entire valley, Amir and the three brothers found themselves posted strategically around Limbung's hut. As had been previously planned Amir stationed himself behind a tree in front, which had a clear view of the entrance. Whichever way Limbung went, it was easy for him to spot and follow his footsteps."

"He waited patiently while mosquitoes buzzed around. In the darkness all he heard were the buzzing, the barking of dogs from afar and the occasional hooting of owls in the forest. After an hour they decided to keep on waiting. Amir fitted an arrow with a green cloth and shot it through a targeted tree. Tariq got the signal. It meant nothing and they had to go on waiting. Tariq signalled Hakim and Eman, likewise. Another hour passed, still nothing. The hour was long and another green arrow was released again. It was an uncertain game of waiting they knew might lead to nothing. Amir was already impatient and time was running. The night was getting deeper and Hana's life was at stake. But what other options did they have when this was the only lead they had?"

"Limbung was inside his hut pacing anxiously. He got up from where he was seated, sat down, walked to the window, pace back and forth, and looked outside anxious of waiting for everybody to be asleep. He was making sure nobody will notice him going out including the people in his household. Oblivious of the eyes trained on him, he decided time had come for him to go out."

"Hundreds of buzzing mosquitoes were swarming over Amir, he had to move every now and then, slapping them with his palm, and weighing at the gravity of what had been happening. He hoped Limbung had nothing to do with this. It would not have come about if he was quick, quick in telling his feelings."

"Amir regretted. Had he announced his feeling for everybody to know, Limbung would not have persisted in pursuing. Our relationship would have served as a deterrent for him and other suitors to pursue. All of what was happening now came into clear perspective. Limbung's scheming character and previous bullying made him the likely suspect, and gave him the conclusion that there was no other culprit but him."

"Midnight was approaching when the village was about to rest and they were still waiting hovering over the suspect's hut. Then his back door opened slowly. A little oil lamp from inside cast a weak light which spread a long shadow on the doorway. Then a scrawny figure slipped outside. His door shut behind, he took the bamboo stairs down to the road. He looked round to see if it was clear then turned left towards Eman's position, walking almost on tiptoe."

"Without wasting a single second Amir fitted another arrow to warn everybody. This time the colour was red. He aimed and released it instantaneously and hit the targeted tree. Eman and the rest were timely advised, each one receiving their signals."

"Amir waited for the rest to come to his side. `Alright let's get going. Remember not to move until he passes Eman,´ cautioned Amir by the time the others regrouped."

`It wasn't hard to believe Limbung was behind all this. All over the village he had the profile of a miscreant being a street guy and a loafer, hanging around with people of questionable character. If he were responsible there is no way he could get away with it. He should answer for his acts.´

"And if something actually happened, Amir was cocksure punishment will be handed down on him. He gritted his teeth."

"When the figure passed Eman's position, they moved fast to follow him, careful to arouse his suspicion. His movements were visible under the light of the moon, walking fast along the river bank. Then his walk became a jog, creating a lengthy distance between them. Amir's heart beat faster. His adrenalin shot up, his blood circulation raised faster than normal."

"Limbung was at a reasonable distance now hunching, slithering against the current of the water. They maintained this distance calculating the risks for him to spot them. When he paused they also paused. Through the moonlight they saw his figure crossing the bridge over to the other side. They wondered what he was up to or where he was going. They were hoping that it would lead them towards what they were looking for. He stopped, looked back then slid into the dark forest by entering the muddy path. As far as Limbung was concerned nothing was ominous about the night, unaware of the eyes tracking him."

`I know this way. We've been here before, Amir. It's a path that goes to the other side. There's only one way. If we followed it we would end up in the same place,´ whispered Tariq.

`Good. Hold still until we're certain everything's clear. Wait for the signal, but be ready for any unforeseen encounter,´ Amir said.

"Copses of trees were thick left and right of the way and low lying bushes made going difficult, they had to raise their bolos in front to fend off any branches low enough to lash at their faces."

"A patch of narrow break in the trees admitted a streak of moonbeams, and Amir spotted Limbung's silhouette trudging up and down the hilly part several paces ahead. He stumbled over a fallen tree, went over, kept his balance then found his way through a beaten path."

"Convinced that he was far ahead, they resumed following, assiduously, with full security that he would not see them behind. The path was dark, wild and thick with undergrowth. The moonbeam was an alleviating contrast in darkness."

"Amir was wondering if Limbung was brave enough to be crossing alone in this forest, in the dead of night and without fear of the wild. If it were not for a greater evil, he would not have done it, nor for anything in this world. So more likely he's going for something more mischievous, or perhaps something more precious than his fear of the dark and wild animals lurking around."

"Somewhere in the middle of the forest, they were looking forward to see a hut, a cabin or a shelter of any kind. Otherwise, where was the crazy Limbung be going? It was a logical conclusion which was clear enough to point in that direction."

"Not long after, Amir could see the end to the clusters of trees leading to an open space past the last of the high trees. Though initially the trees were a safe cover, he was now more than eager to leave it for the revelation and surprise that lay ahead."

"As they penetrated inwards, their efforts were rewarded with a glimmer of hope by the appearance of an outline of a structure in the distance. They edged forward to verify what the outline was. It turned out to be that of a solitary hut in the middle of the clearing. Straining their vision they could see Limbung outside chatting with two men whose presence was strange enough to call for suspicion. What was going on now appeared distinctly clear to Amir.

`Let's split ways. Find out if Hana is inside. If not, we pull out and wait. Timing is the key. If we attack at the same time, they would have no time to react. If she's inside give the signal,´ ordered Amir in the middle of darkness.

"The hut had no windows. Tariq went behind. He saw there was a light coming out from a hole on the wall coming from a small oil lamp. He followed this light creeping slowly nearer, careful not to make loud noises that could attract their attention. Still he heard his footsteps crushing leaves underneath. He could hear his heart beat faster, his breathing withheld. His concentration was on both men guarding and Limbung who was inside and that he should be extra careful. A little blunder could spell the difference. With one eye he peeked inside and saw what he wanted to see. He crept back slowly now certain of what he was doing; he swore to himself he would kill the bastard."

"Amir was already restless waiting. And so were Eman and Hakim."

"When Tariq got back to where he was, he howled like a wolf as loud as he could. They heard the signal and positioned themselves."

"A few seconds later Amir gave the signal to attack."

"The guard on the left heard the second howling and looked up wondering if what he had heard was real. By mere instinct he clutched his weapon on the side. He had no time to take it out from its scabbard. He twitched and a thud was heard on the floor, he even had no time to know what hit him. The arrow Eman had fitted was there stuck on his neck, blood oozing on the ground. Life seemed to have no value for those who made unforgivable acts of disfavour against society."

"At the exact moment, Hakim surged forward with a long spear. The guard on the right stood up to pull his bolo upon seeing the attacker. But Hakim was fast. He released his lance with full force hitting him on the abdomen, the poor guy had no time to resist and fell instantly. Another insignificant life was eliminated by the vanguard of justice."

"Both guards were flat on the ground lifeless and without any movements, this Tariq checked cautiously. They also checked if there were other men around aside from the two."

"At the same time, Amir barged into the hut wielding a bolo. Limbung who was alerted took out his weapon from its side sheath and faced him."

`You imp. Why are you here in this most unwanted moment? You haven't learned your lessons,´ grumbled Limbung.

"Upon hearing the word "imp" Amir's memory of Limbung's bullying came to life and his ears inflamed in anger."

"`I'm asking you the same question, you grumpy fool. Try me now.´ Amir remembered what his father taught him: the blows, the punches and the strikes. He would have no remorse in using them here against this miserable fool."

"Fierce fighting began. Blade against blade sparks glowed in the dim light. Limbung gave a hard blow, Amir waved and sidestepped, surprising Limbung with a right cross. Limbung made a cut but slipped and lost balance. Amir had parried it and returned with a straight to the heart. Limbung fell backwards looking at Amir with an incredulous expression on his face, his eyes dilating. He couldn't believe he was hit. He staggered sideways then his knees gave way. He slumped on the floor his body jerking in spasms. Amir saw he was motionless. He was dead."

"In the dim light, I heard everything. I was in a state of shock and disbelief. My mouth dry, parched, I was shaking all over and shrivelled with cold. I was glad I could see so little. I willed myself not to look at Limbung's eyes, at the blood coming out from his heart, and his lifeless body. Without further ado Amir freed my hands and feet. When I got over it I felt relieved my nightmare was over and I started to sob. I was overjoyed Amir was there to cling to."

"He drew closer to calm me down, with strokes on my hair. It was comforting. Without reservations I flung my arms around him. My emotion was unfathomable Amir was there to cling to. After suffering from the cold of the night it was relieving to feel his warmth ran through my whole body. For a fleeting second in that timeless embrace I wished it were forever."

"Outside, in the middle of darkness, shadows deepened, leaves shuffled, footstalls, and then they barged in, the three brothers Tariq, Eman and Hakim, one after the other. I realized my nightmare had finally ended."

CHAPTER 16

"Our entire household was overjoyed by my rescue, from our housekeepers to my sisters and mother who never stopped raining questions, all of them, who were at the same time aghast at the participation of Limbung."

"My father was grateful. On my return he showed his gratitude by inviting the four men to come for a small thanksgiving feast. It was a small celebration with only the four of them as guests, Lara and the family but abundant with food. Seated at a long table where food and drinks glittered, we lavished at the preparation. There was suckling pig, with a guava fruit stuffed in its mouth. Around it were different servings of pork stew, fried chicken, beef steak, broiled vegetables, white rice, bread and tropical fruits of all kinds. Drinks were served around continuously by attending young maids. Music floated in the air and robins twittered outside".

"Tariq now realized how lucky he was to have been around, seated among the daughters of the Rajah. Had not Limbung made an entirely outrageous mess of himself he would not have been able to dine in this one of a kind gathering of special people in Sandakan. He was proud to have participated in it and he was proud of his two brothers and especially proud of his dear friend Amir. He sat beside his friend smiling contentedly in front of us three sisters."

"Rajah Cali who was at the head of the table stood up and the talking came to a hush . . . then silence."

`My dear friends, it's a pleasure to have your presence tonight. I'd like to express my happiness on my daughter's return by this simple celebration before you. I am especially thankful to you Amir and to you three brothers for your invaluable efforts . . . ´

"It was a short speech but full of meaning and emotions. And after he had spoken and taken his seat Amir rose to say something."

`May I have this rare opportunity to speak in my group's own behalf? My friends and I acted with a sense of duty to our community. We had to do it or nobody else would have done it. It was also on the impulse of a higher respect to you my dear Rajah Cali, being the leader of our village. Alone, I would not have been able to do it. Nor would I have been able to embark on such a risky effort without the help of my friends. It is to Tariq, Eman and Hakim that we should be more grateful to. I am personally thankful to them,´ he paused for a brief moment then continued.

`I must admit my intentions were more personal. I did it because of the greater fear of losing Hana,´ on saying this he turned his gaze at my direction.

"All eyes followed his and shifted on me. I was elated to have heard such inspiring words from him, my heart swooned inside. It was my cheeks which gave my feelings away, turning red. I was blushing and in my silence I wanted to say I was happy he had said those words."

"Then Amir continued, stammering a bit, turning to my father again. He decided time had come for him to be courageous to show his true feelings."

`I could never imagine myself living without her, my dear Rajah Cali. God knows I love your daughter,´ he hesitated, wondering whether he would go on then finally uttered the words, ` I am respectfully asking you, before these who are present, the hand of your daughter as my wife.´

"Then he faced me. I was waiting and hoping he would say it finally. Then I heard him say it."

`My dear Hana, it has been a long time since I wanted to tell you this. Will you marry me and become my wife?´

"On hearing his words I was overwhelmed with an inexplicable joy within me."

"Deep within my heart I wanted to say yes and ran into his arms, but custom and tradition suggested that I should not be too eager to show my feelings, but to wait and act properly for the right time. I was in my seat speechless, simpering, showing my feelings by simply smiling, and he knew it meant a yes answer. My sisters caught this familiar expression who also smiled with approval. Lara wanted to shout. Tariq rejoiced with triumph and so did the rest of his brothers. I loved him too and wished to be his wife."

"The night was tranquil, the moon in perfect harmony, spreading its dazzling splendor across Sandakan. It was a perfect night for romance and the bonding of hearts, and the mood of my father was all out for my happiness. He acceded wholeheartedly and gave his blessings without any questions. He knew Amir would take care of me, certain that he would love me for whatever the cost it may take. This was shown by his noble act of risking his life. There was no question in that anymore."

"Thereafter, arrangements were made, Amir's mother came formally to talk about it with the Rajah, and we were slated to be married. We were bonded together as husband and wife in a ceremony which was attended by no other than the whole village. It was a big double tribal wedding, with Lara and her fiancée being married together with us, accompanied by a huge festivity of eating and drinking and a whole day of merry making. I think that was the happiest day of my life."

"Is that all, Lala . . . the end of your story?" Ilang-ilang inquired inquisitively.

"Hang on my dear child! I still have to tell you what happened afterwards," Lala Hana said, now relieved to have told part of her story.

The night was getting close and they decided to go indoors. She helped her great-grandmother take her steps and in no time were seated inside the *ibuh rumah* on a sofa.

CHAPTER 17

"After the guests had gone and the family tucked in their rooms to rest, the housekeepers took over to turn the place back into its usual order. Amir and I found ourselves seated by the window of my room. Beyond was the moon in the sky and streaks of silvery moonlight slipped through scanty thin clouds which revealed both our happy faces. The mood was totally spellbinding. Absorbed completely by ourselves, we were oblivious of the world outside."

"I felt Amir so close and out of nowhere I asked him, `Where would you want us to live, at your mother's or at home? My father would prefer to see me home, if it would not be an objection to you, *majal* . . . my love. My room is still my room.'"

`Not in any of those places you mentioned, although it would mean no expenses on our part. I'd prefer to live separately and build my own home. I already contracted Hakim to build our house beside mother's hut. For the meantime I would like you to choose. There's a place in Beluran which Tariq offered, belonging to his family. He said it's vacant and we could use it for a week or two. Or we could stay at home with my mother.´

`I think a week away from here is not a bad choice, *majal*.´ He gave me some choices for our honeymoon and far away from Sandakan was the best one for us.

"Presents from friends were all over my room still unopened. I put all of them aside and drew myself closer to Amir. I felt that we deserved to be alone by ourselves where nobody could disturb us after that long celebration. Finally we would be alone by ourselves in a remote place. My imagination flew ahead. I saw him leading the cart and enjoying the short trip to a log cabin in Beluran."

`I have never had a lovely evening. You know tomorrow I would start packing and then off we go.´

`Remember that day after the hurricane?´ he held my hands and looked at me with awe.

`Who would ever forget that?´

`I found you so pretty. But today you are prettier than ever.´

`Oh, Amir.´

`And that's because I have you all by myself now. I love you Hana.´

`I love you too, my dear Amir . . . ever since.´

"The following morning after our wedding we packed and hopped unto the ox driven cart. The cabin was tricky to locate. It was buried in a remote and inaccessible part of the woods, up in the mountains. We had to leave the cart, transfer the luggage on the back of the ox and walk a mile to reach the cabin. From the road it was difficult to see it, for it was covered with high trees and thick bushes. Finally discovering it, it revealed itself as a thatched cabin framed of *dau* logs which stood on a hill, perhaps for decades."

"We opened the door and looked around. It had a musky odor evidently due to long periods of vacancy, dusty but still habitable. With a few cleaning and arranging it would be ready for us to occupy. Amir went to look for food. I knew he would be back later. So I unpacked, prepared the kitchen, lit the torch fire and made the cabin warm for the night."

"Our evenings were the best of all. We bathe, changed, have dinner and talked incessantly about the future and practically about anything. Outside, the wind blew, rustled the leaves and rattled the window flaps but this only gave us the unique feeling of being alone inside, in our own seclusion and wrapped in each other's arms."

"`Amir, are you conscious of comfortable living?´ I whispered in his ears. I was filled with an unfamiliar warmth that flooded my whole being. I had longed to be joined with him, to become one with him, here alone in a faraway place where no one would dare disturb the stillness and tranquillity of the moment."

`I think less about it, if that's what you mean, my dear. But I would want you to live comfortably where you will have everything you need.´

"I snuggled in the tenderness of his embrace, and I whispered, `for me comfort is now, to be with you, and to reach you whenever I want to touch you.´"

`How about having a big house with plenty of rooms, where water is brought to you anytime, where you can do whatever you want to do, cook meals and take shower at the comfort of not fetching water from the spring anymore?´

`Now that's what I call luxury. But, how will it be done?´

`Eman had devised something to conduct water from the spring to our home. I want to see it done. He said he would experiment with the idea when I made the house for us.´

"`I see,´ I heard his explanation but my mind was in the intimacy of the moment, immersed in the sweetness of his presence,"

`*Majal*, since when did you start loving me?´

"Amir thought for a brief moment, and with devouring eyes penetrated deeply into my whole being."

`When I thought I was going to lose you to that imbecile,´ he spoke softly and drowned me with warm kisses.

`And you?´ he pleaded.

`At the time all the girls started talking about you. I thought it would be exciting to join in,´ I giggled, unabashed of what I had just said.

"We locked eyes. I was waiting for him to say something. He moaned and I felt him breathe deeply."

`How about having plenty of children around you,´ he whispered. I was lost in the softness of his voice.

`Oh *majal*, you can have as many as you want,´ was all I could say.

"We were full of love and the whole night belonged to us, time was inconsequential. I buried my head on his shoulder, and felt lost in his arms and kisses. Then I forgot what happened next, bewildered by the ecstasy of the moment. When I awoke in the middle of the night, I felt him beside me and I knew it was a dream no more."

"On our last day, Amir checked everything inside to see if the place was in order, threw the garbage out then locked the door behind. Two weeks, alone by ourselves, seemed so short a time. But that's how honeymoon was, fleeting and perfect as long as it lasted. Now we had to go back to Sandakan to face reality. I knew there will be challenges ahead. For a new couple we had to plan our future and the future of our children."

CHAPTER 18

"Our conjugal house was practically built at no cost at all. All the materials were taken from the forests which were free. Then labour was contributed by most of the single men in the village led by Hakim and Eman. They insisted it was a gift of love for the newlyweds, borne out of unity and the brotherhood spirit, exemplified by centralized teamwork and concerted effort in attaining some worthy goals such as home constructions, which was not uncommon in the culture."

"Our hut was perfect, built exactly at the site where Amir wanted it to be, beside his mother's. It had two bedrooms, a spacious *ibu rumah,* and a conventional kitchen. In place of the bamboo slats, the floor was made of strong *dau* wood, wall to wall. The bathroom and toilet were also installed inside, so that we didn't have to cross a bridge to an outhouse. A little garden at the back was ideally developed for my flowers by Amir himself. It was fenced around by a low inter-netted bamboo slats to keep strangers and wild animals away, with a simple gate for access."

"My happiness in having my own home was immeasurable, matched only by my marriage to Amir. I had full liberty to decorate it with whatever I desired to conform it to my taste. I was the mistress of the house and I wanted it to be as simple and practical as it could be. My dear Amir never changed or touched anything that I labored to make it as comfortable as I wanted our home to be, taking all my decisions with utmost respect."

"Our bedroom was the heart and center of all our activities. This was where we talk, play and plan everything for the future, so I made it a point to change linens regularly. At the sides were two small matching side tables with drawers, where we could put our own personal belongings separately. Beside the curtained window stood an oil lamp on top of a bigger table to illuminate the room. Our clothing was piled neatly on top of each other in a large wooden chest."

"Water was now running from the spring to our simple home, through bamboo poles connected one to each other. The bamboo to bamboo fittings were done with pegs to keep them together. But how to control the water was Eman's most pressing problem, which gave him the headaches: there was no contrivance to stop the flow and let it continue when we needed it, so waste of precious water was unstoppable. He tried a stop-cock made of wood to plug the mouth of the bamboo. But gravity made water to come out at the joints. The idea of a canal through the ground had never found popularity because of its impracticability, so it was discarded right at the start."

"Lack of running water was also the reason outhouses were separated away from the main huts. In older homes people had to cross a bamboo bridge before reaching it, for sanitary reasons; having one inside had never been thought of and was impractical. The obvious reason was the absence of septic receptacles and the unavailability of flowing water for cleaning which had to be fetched from a nearby well, spring or river."

"In spite of this little imperfection it was still considered a novelty and a breakthrough in housing construction. Carpenters and constructors imitated its architecture as a model for modern houses and regarded the idea as an overnight success in innovations."

CHAPTER 19

"Now I drew myself nearer, embraced Amir, and reminded him gently, `If you are going to ask me again, then you know my decision, *majal*. I am against it. I have never wanted you to go and that's final for me.´ I pulled myself apart and started pacing. He sighed. His voice was anxious as he looked at me."

`I know you are but please try to see things from my point of view, *majal*. More than anything else I want to do whatever I can, to make your future and our children's future as secure as you deserve it to be, so I want you to understand me all the way. It would be for your own good and for the good of our future. I love you and this does not alter anything.´

"My heart writhed for him. We have recently been married and now this sudden stroke of decision. Of course he was still young and he had had so much to do for our future. But doing this adventure, and be separated from me in such an uncertain duration of time was hard enough for me to bear."

`It's too risky, and how long would you be away?´

"I took a seat beside him on a bamboo bench, and went on stitching the shirt for our first baby, thinking of how to convince him. I now put it down to reach for his hand and hold it in my own. We were in this mood of uncertainty, then silence permeated. Had I not been on the way, I would have insisted of going with him."

`You must worry at nothing. Sometimes you have to be optimistic. Look into the future,´ he stressed it gently again, walked towards the window and looked at the starry sky with a sigh.

"I was quiet, just stared off."

`Of course I can't avoid worrying,´ I insisted. `So many things might happen and I want to be with you all the time. Only one day of absence might kill me of longing. You are my husband, and it's my right and my wish to be with you every second of my waking time . . . and we're having this.´

"I moved and pulled up, holding my tummy as if trying to protect it from falling. I took a few careful steps and drew myself nearer."

"He turned to face me, hold my hands and held me close. `It is also my desire to be able to prove to you that this is possible, that's why I'm doing this . . . I want to be assured, *majal*, my love, that when I'm away you will take care of yourself. Remember that whatever decisions I made, I made them in the knowledge that I want you to be happy. I wouldn't be long, I assure you. Promise me that.´"

"I nodded curtly and then began pacing the room. I had to nod my head instead of saying something, when tears started to fill my eyes and trickle slowly down my cheeks. He held me close and gave me a kiss on the cheek."

"A light grip of my shoulder signified that Amir was happy of my response. He then reached out for the blue velvet bag he had been keeping and wanting to show me for so long."

`I have a surprise for you. This was treasured so much by *ibu*. My father entrusted it to her for me, for years, until I became prepared to receive it. I'm giving it to you. Open it. I hope you would like it. He glanced at me with a twinkle of joy in his eyes.´

"Slowly, with trembling hands, I loosened the strings, widened the opening and peered inside. Slowly I poured them out."

`Liked it? Oh . . . I love them, *majal*,´ I burst with pleasure as soon as I saw the pearls on my hand.

`What should I do with them?´ I asked him, excited.

`That's the same question I asked my mother when she gave it to me. It will be yours to keep, to remember all the good times and my undying love to you, Hana.´

CHAPTER 20

"The day had broken perfectly. No clouds in the sky and the river flowed placidly. They were also in high spirits, the brothers and Amir; it seemed the weather had cooperated with their plan."

`Let's insert the logs one at a time, guys, starting from the front. At the count of three we lift the boat slowly. Once the last log is placed we start pushing and let it roll,´ ordered Hakim.

"The boat inched bit by bit, finally gliding into the water. It splashed and a cry of joy and triumph followed, all of them patting Hakim at the back for a job well done. The boat bobbed and floated steadily."

"All too soon provisions were gathered to last days of sea voyage. A goatskin was filled with coco red *tubà* wine and another two with drinkable water. Sufficient supply of rice and marinated pork's meat soaked in vinegar and salt were also hauled in. Tariq brought in a bunch of green bananas and a sack of papayas. He knew overnight at sea would ripen them naturally. Amir checked their weapons and fishing equipment assiduously to see they were not forgotten. Personal belongings were limited to one bundle each."

"There were three of them, Amir, Tariq and Eman, so far the first ever. Pioneers would be who were set to embark on an adventure that would take them to a new beginning. Hakim was left behind to care for their mother, besides having a couple of construction projects going on that should be completed."

"The sky was clear and the air breezy but humid. Best time for travel. Villagers young and adults were there lining the riverbanks to see the men off, majority of them were plainly curious. We were there too, my sisters and father among the crowd. Raja Cali had to be there to bid them good bye."

"Tears brimmed in my eyes. Amir who saw this moved closer and held me tightly. He smiled as the memory of making love the night before commanded his thoughts and lingered in his mind. He teased me on this."

`Don't worry. We'll be back before you know it. Please do take care of *ibu*,´ assured Amir in a whisper.

`We'd better be going. Push the boat, Hakim. The rest start rowing,´ ordered Amir to his companions.

"They did as told, rowing laboriously until they gained speed, the boat gliding smoothly down into the middle of the river. It wobbled then recovered balance in no time, and slithered through the waters."

"Amir looked at the tall coconut trees that dotted the banks as they raced by. He was grateful of their existence, and their usefulness, admiring their role in the lives of the village people for as long as he could remember: they were the source of oil for their lamps; soap for washing; food and *tubá;* the leaves used as rooftops; the trunks as stilts and frames of their huts; and the husks for firewood. He was forever thankful to these magical tropical trees, the source of life. The reasons for their existence or why they existed nagged his thoughts. Nature had a strange way of making life easier, he contemplated."

"He looked back to see that the crowd was dispersing and getting thin. When they took the curve we lost sight of them completely. I lost sight of him. Who would ever know when I would see him again?"

`We'd be at the mouth before sunset, and out into the broad sea. Let's hope the *Ginoos* will be merciful,´ Amir looked at the sky in silent prayer.

`Look . . . that's where we catch fish, ´ pointed Tariq at the exact site, `they say it's where the sweet water meets the salt water.´

"When they moved out into the wide sea, they saw the last vestiges of the setting sun on their right. Their rowing was continuous, the sound monotonous. All they perceived was the lapping of the waves, the crushing of water on their sides and the sound of the paddles as they cut through the waters. They stayed in this direction without changing left or right ways, towards the mountains they had seen from the river, straight ahead towards an island they never knew."

"The night came to a close and darkness hovered over. Providence must have been steering the boat as the moon showed no light behind the clouds. It was pitch dark. For a moment Amir was wondering if they did the right thing, leaving their loved ones behind and the easy life, heading towards the unknown."

CHAPTER 21

"The first light of dawn came out from the horizon, fresh with so much promise and with it the steady movement of the boat about to reach land. From their position they could breathe the warm air from land coming their way and marveled at the line of the shore which was getting thicker and nearer. They landed on the sandy shore, dropped anchor, fastened moorings then disembarked. Tariq kneeled down bowed his head and kissed the ground, thanking the *Ginoos* of this new found land."

"He prepared breakfast in high spirits, humming his favorite tune. When they had had enough, they roamed about and delighted their eyes with all things new. Losing no time they took their long spears and bows out and started for the quarry which was aplenty. Hunting was never as hard as they anticipated. When they saw they had sufficient meat, they went back to the beach and laid on the sand to rest."

`There are countless of things to discover in this island. Let's see if we find people first. Now, let's split ways. Don't mess up with them, and then come back as soon as you reach the end,´ ordered Amir after an hour's rest.

"It took each one of them days to reach the other side and days to come back to their original position. First to return was Eman. While waiting for the others he set up camp for the night. He gathered fallen coco leaves on the ground, stitched them together and built a make shift roof. When Amir arrived he prepared supper and waited for the rest to come."

`I saw no significant thing on my side, except the sea. Not a soul. Only wild birds which flew away once they saw me coming,´ related Eman.

`I reached the end. I had climbed up a hill which led me to a cliff overlooking the other side and stretched my vision. I'm positive I saw the shape of a boat in the distance, moored on the rocky shore. But I could make out no life whatsoever. There was no movement, so I crept low and ran back as fast as I could,´ reported Tariq.

`Very well . . . tomorrow you will lead us back to where you saw it, Tariq. To the north I found no humans, only boisterous monkeys swinging from tree to tree, and all kinds of tropical birds of different colors, scampering away as I approached,´ related Amir, while cleaning his bolo.

"Supper was passed around a bonfire. The salty air was humid but fresh, blowing lightly from the sea. After enjoying the meal of pork's meat Amir shared what he had been thinking all the while."

`Did I tell you my *ayah* was here before?´

`I remember you telling me that story. Besides everybody in Sandakan heard of that story from other people, it has become lore,´ Eman assumed.

`My *ibu* told me it's true. He was the first to come . . . and alone.´

`There are no traces, though,´ said Tariq.

`Yah, there should have been at least something that would tell us he was here,´ interjected Eman.

`I have. And I left it with Hana. They were twenty eight beautiful golden pearls from the sea; I wondered which part of this island he found them.´

"A tick of a moment ensued when silence interrupted the conversation to let Amir's revelation sink in."

Then he opened up. `I had been thinking of giving a name to this island since we landed. Haven't you thought so likewise? It would be proper to solicit your opinions first. I know you may have a better one on your mind, especially you Eman who could easily come up with good ideas.´

`Hmmm. . . Let me think. We could name this the Step stone Island,´ stated Eman, brimming with pride on his word.

`It sounds fitting and logical, considering that we would be using this as a stepping stone to that bigger island in the north. But let's think of some more names. A name that is tribal sounding and significant perhaps,´ Amir shifted a leg.

`How about *Tambasakan*,´ joked Tariq, giving reference to a kind of fish they used to catch at the mouth of the river.

`Or The Pearl Island,´ said Tariq, shifting his position, now more serious.

`I'd reserve my suggestions until I came up with a better one, then we decide tomorrow,´ whispered Amir already about to slide into sleep.

"Old folks used to say bright ideas usually come out from a rested body and a sound mind; they were so exhausted their eyelids would not open anymore. Their conversation came to inaudible murmurings, then silence. No words came out from anyone, so they chose to lie on their backs to rest for the night."

"Another dawn broke in, morning came and they got up fresh. After having breakfast they washed themselves up and went to the bushes for their personal needs, and they were ready to go."

"Tariq was ahead, leading them. On the hilly side they laid low and crept like a crocodile. The cliff had a good view of the sea. Without any mistaking, the boat was there bobbing among the waves. They inched their way, hiding among rocks and bushes, their safety was primary. Bolo in hand they sprang forward and ran as fast as they could to take advantage of surprise."

`Not a soul.´

"They found nobody, only monkeys who jumped out on seeing them, surprised as they were. Evidently the animals were there to scourge for food."

"The boat was a throve of treasures: they found cooking utensils, pans, clay pots, spears and bows, bundles of clothing, jars of honey and spices and preserved food. The boat itself was intact and still sea worthy. On its side was written the word SULU."

`Where could the people be from and why was the boat abandoned,´ they wondered, scanning farther out to inquire.

`Hey look!!! Come,´ shouted Eman who found something.

"They hurried to his side instantly, running in fact."

`Look . . . a skeleton. There's another one on that side. Two of them,´ hollered Tariq excitedly.

`There must be more of them. The rest must have died in the sea and thrown overboard,´ Eman surmised with some calculations.

"One of Eman's earliest memories was when he was about twelve years old. They were on the seashore, the sky was clear and the air from the sea was hot and sticky. His father used to take him to harvest edible clams which were all over the shore when the tide was low and sea water was up to his ankles. All they had to do was to dig the ground where they were hidden, pick the shells and fill his basket full of them. Inside the clamshell was sweet meat, they used to bring home as part of their meals."

"They were combing the beach when a raft coming from the high seas landed without notice. His father told him to run and call for help. But when he looked back he saw that his father was already fighting with the five short, black men who had disembarked from the raft. They had kinky hair and they were armed with long spears."

"When help came it was already too late. His father's body was floating on the water; the attackers had already been gone."

"The boat people came from the same tribe who took his father's life. They were sea marauders, pirates or seafarers: People who came from the other big neighboring islands with dark skin, kinky hair, belonging to the `Ita´ tribe, and known to be itinerant who roamed around. A satisfactory explanation of their mysterious death could not be explained, seeing that there were no signs of violence in the skeleton, or why they were stranded in that island. Perhaps they died of a plague, Eman only guessed. He had long forgotten what they had done to his father. All he remembered now was how they looked from far away- short resembling midgets, the same size as the skeletons they have found in the island."

`Let's go back to Sandakan and tell our story about this discovery. I'm certain they would be interested to know. Besides, I already missed my family,´ decided Amir.

`We can use this boat, Amir. It's bigger and sturdier,´ suggested Tariq.

`Wait. Don't you think it's best to smoke it first, to drive away bad spirits?´

`Yeah, let's light some coco leaves and place them around the boat.´

"They gathered dry coconut leaves in a pile then set fire to it."

"As soon as the smoking was terminated they sailed back to Sandakan. Over time the island had been referred to as SULU by association to the boat people. Objections were muted especially from Tariq and Eman. Sulu was nevertheless tribal sounding, which was what they wanted in the first place."

CHAPTER 22

"Amir's absence was painful. It took me shortly though to swing back to my old room in the big house, leaving the home where we lived to the dusts. Although the occupants for the meantime were undesirable, I regularly made a cursory look at it every day to check. When the furniture needed dusting I personally took care of it at the insistence of our housekeepers who were eager to help. I was looking forward to his coming one day, and I wanted no other people to touch them for sentimental reasons."

"One early morning, which I usually do to check, I got a shock of my life when the lock which was used to keep away intruders was smashed. My heart beat faster to see the door open. I pushed it slowly and went inside. It was ransacked. The drawers to the cabinets were strewn everywhere, the bed turned over, a vase was broken and the chairs were upside down. I went back home to my father and reported the incident. Rajah Cali came and saw the mess."

`Hmm . . .who would ever do this to you?´ With arms folded on his breast, my father surveyed the intrusion with a hawkish eye.

`I couldn't think of anybody so cruel, *ayah*.´

`Does Amir have any enemies?´

`None that I could think of.´

`Did you check thoroughly if you had lost anything of value? The looks of it, they were looking for something valuable.´ He eyed everything carefully to get any clues.

`The only valuable things that we have are the pearls. But they are always with me. I don't leave them here in Amir's absence.´

`It's clear now that they were after those pearls. Tell Ondo to help you arrange everything back to where they were.´

`I'll check if Amir's mother's safe in the other hut.´

"Father walked off leaving me behind to contemplate and assess the damage. My father wasted no time to check if she was alright. In a few minutes he came back with her."

`Oh, my God! What's happening here?´ *Ibu* exclaimed, unbelieving of all the disorder that met her eyes.

`Someone came to search for something, taking advantage of Amir's absence, *ibu*.´

`It was unprecedented and therefore alarming.´

`There's always a first time, *ibu*. And they were looking for the pearls.´

`Precisely what I guessed,´ she said, `were they able to get them?´

`Luckily, they were all with me. I wonder what Amir would say to learn that I lost them.´

`Good thing nobody was hurt.´

"So far, it never happened again. I knew some people were interested in them and the value they get in the market. Some were interested in their legendary power, the power which gave your great grandfather Kusgan the facility to crush all his enemies with his bare hands. Its value alone was tempting enough for other scheming greedy sloths to be interested."

"The presence of the twenty eight golden pearls was no secret in Sandakan and people learned of their existence by word of mouth. Whichever the reason was, it was now clear that those pearls have some intrinsic values that kept people's imaginations whirling to acquire them."

CHAPTER 23

"So what became of Tariq's brothers, lala?"

"They had their own families, Hakim with five children and Eman, six."

"Due to the movements of people to Sulu and the peninsula up north, demand for the boat rose rapidly, and the need for a bigger, stronger and safer ones gave life to a lucrative industry for the people, especially to Hakim, who knew the boat construction ahead of the others. Innovations were made to the original sketch, improving it considerably. Orders kept coming and many villagers were benefitted in employment."

"Eman made a name for himself, too. Water conduction became popular and demand rose many folds over. Every time Hakim got a contract for a new house, his water system was attached as an essential part of the project. Control of the flow which had been a nagging problem had been sorted out eventually."

"It seems Mr. Luck had smiled on all of them," Ilang-ilang commented.

"Yeah, he was hoping he could find other materials aside from the bamboos. This never stopped him from investigating. He never knew stone walls or aqueducts had already been used to conduct water to castles in other places in the west. He started experimenting with it."

"Not only this. The water that got into everybody's homes needed an exit after using. So the two brothers had to devise something that could drain all the dirty used up water towards the river. This was another source of employment."

"Then there was the septic tank, so that outhouses became outmoded and gone to be replaced by the toilets in newly constructed houses."

"Tariq remained single all his life and chose to be at the side of Amir and working hand in hand with us and remaining to be an ever loyal friend."

"As you well know your Lolo Amir became Sandakan's Rajah. His reign was so far peaceful and prosperous with so many businesses cropping up all over the village. His adventurous character made him push further to the north of Zulu and conquer more territories and owning vast track of lands."

"More Sandakan villagers learned to cross the sea to Sulu Island which was eventually made a stepping stone to a peninsula further north. Trade flourished as more and more young people ventured out to seek new land and adventure. Copra and rice changed hands freely. Migration rose rapidly, pushing people further to the neighboring islands in the north. Also, Sulu became an interesting destination because of its precious golden pearls which could only be found in its seas."

"Decades of years since then had passed, so many events had happened and time stood still when our love survived the test of time."

"Then one ordinary day turned into a test of character and fortitude, when we found your Lolo weak in bed. He could stand up no more nor raise his hand, his eyeballs rolling around in their sockets. The village medicine man concluded that a bad spirit entered his body. All medicines, herbs and prayers were tried but his situation only changed a little. The once strong, spirit had left his body. The once strong Amir was now no more than a weak old body depreciated and emaciated that would take in no food anymore. All his friends had left him years before. Now it's time for him to follow, concluded the medicine man."

"But he was wrong. Lolo's mind was still strong. He struggled. But his body won't let him. In agony I fed him fluids, washed him and stayed close in his bed, for days and weeks. It extended to months."

" One day we were all around him: The village medicine man, our children and grandchildren, and most of Sandakan's influential people. The medicine man was there, giving him the last unction to shorten his sufferings. They wanted him to rest in peace. He smoked his bed and said a lot of prayers. The final hours came."

"His eyes closed his breathing deep and heavy and he was fighting inside. The prayers went on and the smoking subsided, his breathing became slow until he heaved a deep sigh. His breathing stopped. And we knew he had left us."

Grief is torture. Pain permeated all over followed with gnawing numbness. No feeling of remorse, only love. There's nothing to hold on to but sadness and the memories of life's blessings, having been snatched away and held far in time. One can do nothing but be shifted towards compassion.

"I headed upstairs, walked down the corridor and paused at the door to our bedroom. It was now empty. I looked around the room at the familiar objects, each one striking a chord of unique associations, of the times I spent with Amir. My scanning eyes finally rested on the bed we used to share. So many conversations, plans for the future and much pleasure had transpired there."

"I closed the door slowly and walked down the corridor and back to where Amir was laid. I met compassion and love from my children and grandchildren, who were around him. Your lolo's efforts were never futile. He had made all of them capable of standing on their own two feet. He died with hopes fulfilled. Our six children, your uncles and aunts, are well provided as you pretty well know. And so are all of your cousins."

"Both Hakim and Eman died prosperously. My two sisters Sampa and Guita both married fellow Sandakan villagers and lived separate happy lives with so many children who have grown up. Some of them travelled to as far as to the islands towards the north."

"How about Rajah Cali?" asked Ilang-ilang.

"Oh . . . he died ahead of everybody . . . in old age."

CHAPTER 24

Only those who had seen her younger days could tell who great-grandma Hana was in her last remaining years. She had gained a lot of weight at the sides, in front and on her face. Her hair streaked with ashen shades of gray held together in a bun. But her features still revealed her once youthful years. She's one hundred years old but had none of the infirmities of the aged. Great-grandma walked with a stick. Her bones ached, but still in command of her faculties.

She had grieved at the passing of her Amir; the sorrow that came over was indescribable. She loved him as a friend and as the father of her six children. As the Rajah of his people, she believed that the goodness in him was what made him unforgettable: he fed the hungry, helped those who were distressed, fought for other people's right and was the best husband she ever had.

Now alone, great-grandma Hana's remaining consolation was her love for those who were left behind and most especially to her grandchildren. During Ilang-ilang's brief stay she developed a special fondness to her. That span of a little time they spent together made them closer. Ilang-ilang believed it's because they saw each other less that she had gained a special affection to her. The story of her life made them closer which tied the bond tightly together. This left her a little reluctant to be leaving Sandakan and returning to the relative calmness of Opon, with her parents, her hometown. And now she had to bid her goodbye.

"Ilang-ilang, dear, it has been a lovely vacation with you around. When do you think you would be back?" great- grandma whimpered and croaked.

"Lala, I would be back someday when time and the sea would permit me to travel. It would also all depend on *Tata* and *Nana*. It was truly a memorable summer. And the story. . . it was unforgettable." Ilang-ilang was getting ready to go and all her folded dresses and things were on top of the table, all set up to be arranged into her travelling bag.

"I wish to see that day. My heart tells me you'd become a pretty lady who'd be admired by so many men. I hope to see you first before you get married, my dear child." Great-grandma Hana moved towards her from where she was seated.

"By that time I would come back with a surprise for you, Lala. I haven't thought about it yet but when it comes you will be the first person to know. I would never fall into such things unless I come for your blessing. And that's a promise," Ilang-ilang said honestly, and then started to put all her things inside.

"I'd be waiting for that time, my dear Ilang-ilang."

"Tell me Lala. Why is it that my *Nana* doesn't feel like coming back to Sandakan anymore? That has been a mystery to me for a long time," Ilang-ilang looked far away through the window past her.

"It's a long story, my dear. It's about her running away with your father. Nobody in Sandakan had ever approved of their relationship."

"I see. Why were they against it?" she finished packing then closed her bag.

"Nobody liked your father. He was so fierce and got into trouble most of the time, but your *nana* loved him so much. What could we do? So they ran away and ended up in that island where you are now living, away from all the relatives. Look at them now . . . and look at you."

Ilang-ilang's mother's stubbornness never affected great-grandma though. She had always been fond of her in spite of her unconventional ways. Her going away with Ilang-ilang's father affected most of her siblings and most gravely to her father who lost his life trying to stop them.

Ilang-ilang's stay had come to an end and she was leaving, about to go back to where she came from. It's a family tradition to send her something of a gift to the people at home- a tradition of giving among family members. Great-grandma Hana had one for grandma. For the rest of the people, only a basketful of durian fruits.

She reached for her possession and took out the velvet bag she had been keeping and wanting to show Ilang-ilang during her brief stay. She straightened her back, legs together, assuming her usual poise, a poise that was controlled and royal. There was a noble way in the way she held her head and her general deportment, worthy of being the daughter of a Rajah.

"Now, here's something that I'd like you to give to your grandma. I hope these would give her long life and happiness, as they have given me all these years. Please tell her to take good care of them with the same love and care I have given them."

"And never forget to tell your mother that if she's willing to come back to Sandakan the house is open for her. Tell her."

"I will Lala Hana . . ."

The velvet bag had faded through the years and was frayed at the seam. Ilang-ilang opened it to look inside then held it firmly tucked in her possession. They were the twenty eight lustrous golden pearls Lala Hana told her in her story.

"Yes, they are without doubt beautiful, Ilang-ilang. I'm not sure if I could still last some years more to be keeping them safe with me, so I'm bequeathing them to your grandma."

She smiled at her great-grandma and said, "I'll keep them for her, Lala." She left her seat and involuntarily picked up her bag, then drop it again on the floor to embrace her Lala Hana.

She had a promise made, and intended to fulfill such promise. Time would only tell when, for she would be back to fulfill such promise in her great-grandma's last remaining years. She had learned life was full of unfulfilled promises thereby breaking the hearts of people. On the other hand there were those which were complied with and made hearts happier. It's a subtle *quid pro quo,* which always ends in either way, never failing. We always hope for the best of either way like the seasons that always turn around, promising cold or warmth to come, the day which promises the night, after pain comes happiness, then those that come from people with a vow to fulfill. She had hers to keep and great-grandma expected her to keep it.

Ilang-ilang kissed great-grandma, Lala Hana, on the cheek, got into the boat which was waiting to take her to Sulu, jumping from island to island and back to the place where she grew up to become the stunning young woman that she was now evolving.

King Macachor

Year 1519

CHAPTER 25

It was in the late middle ages when the port of Seville was buzzing with activities, and folks of all walks were in a hurry. Restaurants and bars brimmed with customers. The harbor was full of anxious and hopeful faces of men who toil on both ends to meet deadlines, working day and night. Still they seemed not to end at all.
Even in the evenings under the hazy light of torches, the harbor was burning with activities over mountains of boxes and crates, of all sizes, waiting to be distributed and hauled into the five galleons, boxes and crates which contained provisions of food and wine, uniforms, ammunitions, weapons, linens and medicines. They were either hand carried or rolled over depending on their sizes and weights, for there was no other way to haul them into the galleons.

On closer look, sweating muscled stevedores heaved sacks of flour, rice and lentils on their shoulders including baskets of fruits and vegetables, balancing the planks to the second deck to put them in store. Their shoulders thick, their hands calloused of their continuous labour. There was no end to the roaring for they were the real movers.

Summer was in full blast and the heat was unbearable. The banks of Guadalquivir were jam-packed with sunbathers lying on the grasses hoping to get some tan, some were pouring on their favorite books under the shade of colorful parasols, children were playing, and girls and boys were tromping in the water to cool themselves up. Nobody stayed in their homes to escape the searing heat. Those who preferred not to be in the river banks were seated around tables in terraces drinking *horchatas* (tiger nut milk), and *gazpacho* fresh drinks. The port was swarming with uniformed soldiers waiting for
their deployment and assignment, as well as eager galleon crews who were getting ready for the well-known sea voyage. It had become a magnet to all kinds of people from all over, who were hoping to be part and witness of a lifetime event that would mark the country in world history.

Jonas Martin was one of the young lads in Seville with an eye for adventure. Like the rest, he had great hopes in joining one of the galleon voyages across the ocean and had always been fascinated by stories told by those who came back and brought fortunes of gold and booties. His hopes had always been scuttled because of his age. Timing was on his side now, having turned twenty one years old and with no legal impediments that could hinder this ambition of travelling. Nor his parents who were adamant and had been against such an idea could prevent him from pursuing this dream. So when he heard that King Charles the fifth had commissioned and financed an exceedingly ambitious mission to the Far East, he lost no time to get a place in this once in a lifetime opportunity. It was no easy feat, though.

Many young men aspired to travel and applied. Chances were awfully small. Competition was stiff. Had he joined the naval force and be part of the crew his chances would have been better, but this was too late at the present circumstance. Deadline for inscription had already lapsed. The only chance he had was to be a part of the second ranked crews doing menial jobs such as cleaning and the kitchen, preparing food for the crew members which he didn't mind doing at all. Still this would not guarantee him a place in the galleons that were sailing.

A month before the scheduled departure Jonas went to the recruitment office to see if he made it. When he arrived he saw many young people milling outside. Some were inside who had come earlier to inquire. He made the line and patiently waited. There were happy sounds from those who found their names. After reading the final list on the bulletin he found out his name was not one of those lucky ones. He read the list over and over. His hopes were dashed again.

Jonas brushed away the word *discourage* from his mind. "This must not deter me from pursuing it," he told himself. "There must be a way. Some people whom I knew, who could lend me a hand to get inside, a connection perhaps. But who?" His mind started to work to retrieve all the names of friends and relatives that could possibly help him.

Juan Serrano's name flashed in his mind. He had heard his uncle would be one of the five captains. So he checked the list again and to his delight found his name was there alright. He was his only chance and talking to him might find him a way, so without wasting any time he walked straight to his office.

His office was lodged in a huge red bricked baroque building in the center of town. The affluent aura it reflected pasted a secured optimism that his connection was indeed weighty, and one of the most important in town. Jonas stood outside hopeful. Looking at the facade, he took the stairs up to the first floor and knocked on a heavy mahogany door. The sweet smile of his young secretary met him as the door opened. She was kind enough to lead Jonas to her desk offering him a seat in front to wait. He sat across from her. He had been here with his mother on several occasions but his eyes still lingered around. On the walls hang pictures of the 1400 era by *Giotto* and *Cimabue*. The décor and the furniture had come with the place. He looked down and saw that the marbled floor was well polished. Nervous and fretting, he never realized he was rubbing his hands. It was only his uncle, he thought, "but why am I so nervous?" There were some magazines on the table so he picked one pretending to read, but his concentration was nowhere other than on the purpose for which he came for. After a minute the secretary ushered him inside.

His uncle Juan's office smelled of tobacco. Old books were stacked on a shelf on his left. On the right stood a lighted oil lamp. There was a painting of *Jan Van Eyck* hanging on the wall behind his desk. He had been writing. Lodged between his fingers was a pen he automatically dropped when he saw Jonas over his spectacles.

"*Buenas noches, tío,*" Jonas said, smiling as he was shown inside his office.

"*Buenas noches*, Jonas," his uncle beckoned him to come forward.

"I see you're alone. Your mother . . . how's she?" he inquired, offering Jonas a chair to sit, indicating it with his right hand.

His uncle Juan was grumpy with balding hair. His eyes were as sharp as a knife when he looked at you. They were only softened when they were behind those glasses he wore for reading. He was his mother's eldest brother, who remained single at the age of fifty. So dedicated to his profession that getting married or having a family was only second to all his future plans.

"She's at home. I decided to come alone, myself."

"Something's wrong? How urgent is your business that you haven't brought her along?"

By the tone of his voice Jonas sensed formality, too serious at this time, to be bothered with petty matters, so it seemed. He gathered all the courage he had to say, what he came for and without any deviations.

He said, "it is indeed urgent. And I know you are the only person who could help me."

"Is it about money, Jonas?" He was eyeing him suspiciously.

"No, *tío*. I came because I know you are the only person who has the capacity to do it."

"Mm. . . How confident are you that you are approaching the right person?"

"Well, I was at the enlistment office and saw your name under *Santiago*. You know how I wanted to be in one of those galleons, *tío Juan*, to travel and see places."

"Get to the point."

"I applied as one of the second rank crew, in fact, hoping to be listed as a kitchen assistant. It was too late for me to be enlisted in the naval force so I tried this way. But my name did not appear in the final list. And the galleons are sailing in a month's time."

"Did you check at the office and ask for reasons?"

"There was no way to do that with the long queue. I read the list several times and came up with your name."

"I see . . . you came here to ask me some favor, to twist somebody's arm or change his name to yours so that you'll be inserted in the list, is that right," his uncle sounded displeased now, his smile turned tight.

"Not in such manner. But if there's a way, short of doing what you have just mentioned," the poor Jonas felt his feet losing balance, too weak to support himself, and a streak of cold sensation ran down his spine.

He recognized his uncle's steadfastness and unbending character, and saying "no" had become second nature to him. Over the years, success in his profession had only served to reinforced these qualities, so now it was almost impossible to deal with him on any level of reason.

"Go home Jonas. It's beyond my powers to accommodate you. The list is final and I see no reason to change it. There's no way you can insult your uncle further. Be a good boy and go home. Your mother will be wondering where you are now," he snarled.

Jonas left. He knew he could not argue with his uncle anymore.

His `no´ answer hit another blow. He could do nothing and it was final, he enunciated those words clearly, his rejection kept ringing in his head. By the time he negotiated the stairs down to the ground floor his heart was heavy with uncertainty. "It's final...I couldn't do anything......it's final." He left the building with his words echoing on the walls. The sky turned gloomy, which got him to thinking for ways. He had the burning desire in his heart, a desire which was fortified by faith, pushing reasons aside that inspired him to carry on. There must be a way. Now he was even more determined than ever.

Jonas' faith was unwavering. If he could change his insignificant penniless life in Seville then this would be his chance. Staying in his hometown would not guarantee him a comfortable future because there was nothing. No jobs even for those who were well prepared. The galleon was his only chance.

He headed home with the same spirit of determination, kicking an empty can as if playing football. He liked playing football. In the middle of the way he changed his mind and decided to postpone home, diverting his direction to the pier where the galleons were anchored. His firmness was inflexible.

Jonas was in a quandary and never had any ideas as to what to do. He sat in one of the crates to contemplate, positioned himself so that he could see the movements of the people, the goings in and out of the crews and the hauling of cargoes, the humming continuous. His head was empty, his mind numb, he couldn't think correctly. He simply wanted to stay there and hoped to find any possibilities, to reflect on how he could change the course of that damn destiny. He was looking for any flaws in security, some inconsequential lapses or relaxation of controls.

Several huge boxes were hauled onto the upper deck, he observed. These were boxes used to contain the provisions, food and drinks, and ammunitions. There were also muscled stevedores hauling sacks of grains on their shoulders unmindful of his presence as if he was a statue devoid of life. The humming and buzzing were in his midst.

Horse drawn carriages came and went to drop cargoes. One particular carriage with a huge auburn stallion stopped immediately in front of where he was sitting. The horse snorted and made a piss on the ground, while the coachman waited for the passengers to alight. It smelled grassy urine, greenish and interminably voluminous. The coach heaved after being freed of the two men who got off to the ground. They pulled a small box made of oak then hefted it away to be hauled into one of the ships.

Two checkers with clipboards and pencils were at the entrance to make sure the quantities being taken in were authorized or correct.

"This is from the office of Captain Juan Serrano," Jonas overheard one of the men who was bringing the box pronounced it with authority.

"What's inside," one of the checkers tapped the box with his pencil, inquiring.

Actually we know nothing. We were only instructed to deliver it to his cabin."

"It's for The Chief Commander Ferdinand Magellan," volunteered one of the men.

It was made of oak, strong and hard, and was used to resist insect and fungal attack because of its high tannin content. He had one at home so he knew its durability. This box was especially made to protect its content from long sea travel. It was one by one span thick and stood about three spans. And on the sides was written *"Fragile This Side Up"*. On one side, *"Receiver: The Chief Commander."*

Special care was given to it by the two men. This aroused his curiosity. Later he would learn that only a few crew members knew its content and it made the more mysterious being specifically to be delivered to the Commander-in-chief only or to any of his trusted men, the captains of the five galleons. It was carried with extra care, and in the seams, where lines were formed by the edges Jonas saw some reddish glow coming out, unnoticed by those carrying it. It would have appeared to be one of those ordinary boxes if he hadn't seen the iridescent light coming out. Mystified, he was wondering what was glowing inside; his imagination flew, until his attention was diverted back to his original purpose in coming to the docks.

He looked at the galleons again. Their sheer size amazed him so much. He walked towards the bow then back to the stern. Measuring from one end to the other, he noticed that there was a curve from bow to stern, which formed the body of the ship. This created a blind spot if he stood on either end. He studied the possibilities and saw that there was something he could do, realizing he actually had several options at his disposal. "I would take the chances, jump on board at the bow's end and hide in the hold between boxes," he mused with excitement, his hopes renewed. On the way home he was already pondering on the execution of his plan, the procedure for which it had to be carried out, and the pros and cons. He would hop on board, under the noses of those guards and hold still until the ship would already be at a safe distance.

    Jonas believed being scrupulous was a virtue. This gave him the cushion to the idea that the act for which he would be doing was non-punishable. He knew running away from home was common among youngsters, but stowing away in a ship was never heard of. If there was a law or regulation which controlled those who slipped into ships then he would be in a big mess. But there was none. If there was, then it would be for not paying the boat fare. In this voyage nobody had to pay for any fare. It was exploratory and all expenses had already been paid by the King. So he bought the logic that he could get away with what he was contriving.

CHAPTER 26

Nabilah was at the kitchen cutting vegetables to prepare lunch, steam was coming out from the rice in one pot and soup was in another. An exceptionally dependable sort of a person, she wore a turban around her head to keep her hair tucked inside, as if that alone would ensure cleanliness in the kitchen. When everything was ready she would call out for the whole family to come down and sit at the table to share the succulent meals she had prepared. Her family worked for the Datu Lapu-lapu, Ilang-ilang's father. Her husband took care of the garden and her daughter to clean the house. She was happy and proud in her work.

Ilang-ilang came out of her room then edged her way to the door of the kitchen. At eighteen, she had become a full blown woman, amazingly pretty, respectful and loving. "Yaya Nabilah tomorrow is Sunday and I'm going to Sugbo to visit grandma. Please, prepare something for me to bring her."

"Do you have anything in your mind?" she calmly inquired.

"Actually I was thinking of bringing her some mangoes."

"It's up to you, my dear child. Fruits would be ideal, considering that she's not too keen on cooked food from here. Besides she cooks her own food." She bustled about, clattering pots and pans.

"Please prepare me a whole basket of yellow mangoes, *Yaya*."

"They're going to be ready before you go." Yaya Nabilah wiped her hands with her apron, and then chopped the ten fresh trout on the table into three parts each.

"Thank you, *Yaya*. I'm confident grandma would love them," her eyes brightened.

"Has she found somebody to live with her yet?" Yaya Nabilah asked, still chopping the fish.

"*Nana* is thinking of sending one of the girls."

"By the way, how old is your grandma?" she asked, then picked up the cut fish with her finger and tossed them into the boiling cauldron. There was warmth in her voice and her face relaxed, showing love and concern.

"She is eighty three. *Nana*'s truly worried about her situation. She said she should not live alone anymore, but grandma's too resolutely obstinate."

"Do you feel the same way?" Yaya Nabilah moved with expert dexterity to cut the onions and tomatoes into slices and introduced them into the boiling water with the fish.

"I want her to be with us. This house is definitely big enough for another person to share it with," while saying this her eyes roamed around the house to demonstrate its enormity.

"And there's an extra room ready for her," seconded Nabilah.

"Well, you know her reasons already. I've seen how she disagreed with your *Tata*'s policies and way of thinking." Nabilah added chopped carrots
and the cabbages to complete the fish soup.

"She has deeper reasons than those, Yaya."

"My mother-in-law had a heart attack and she was never the same again," revealed Yaya Nabilah.

"You have told me nothing about that before."

"She lives with us now and she has the best room in the house: It has a window fronting the sea. Your yayo Akmal's life now is in a hell. Aside from the work he's doing in the garden, he had to take care of her, clean her room and wash her every day. I'm stressed out too. He should be thankful he has me to help him with the housework or he'll be wracking his nerves out." A faint smile came out from her, with a bit of sarcasm.

This apparently cut the story short. Yaya Nabilah returned to her cooking and Ilang-ilang to her room. Before she turned to leave, she left some encouraging words to lighten her Yaya's heart.

"I'm sorry, Yaya. I could see how strenuous it would be for both of you to be living with somebody as delicate as his mother. Your kindness will bring some fruits someday. How old is she, Yaya?"

"She's as old as your grandma, at eighty three."

Yaya Nabilah tossed a pinch of salt into the soup, and turned to look away. Her face had grown weary all these years but the trust that she had gained from working with the family was beyond measure.

CHAPTER 27

Seville in 1519 was a busy port, but with little future for upcoming youngsters. There were no jobs and no chances for improvement which drove most of them to petty crimes and violence. It was the country's golden age and the Spanish armada's dominance of the sea, but in so many ways paradoxical and inconsistent with the life of the masses where the gap was wide and prominent, and so too was Seville's , swarmed with beggars, thieves and the penniless who were lured into the luxury of the galleons.

On the night before the galleons left, Jonas pondered so much then made his decision. The air coming from the sea was hot and humid in the middle of August and the guards were bored and drowsy. That was the opportunity he was looking for, so he hitched a rope to the bowsprit then scaled the portside, climbing step by step, careful not to be seen by the guards. He was glad it was in the middle of darkness. Now or never, it was his only chance. He could slip and fall into the water or be caught. His desire was stronger it made fear smaller. He hopped in. By the time he got on board Jonas slid himself into the lower deck and crouched among the cargoes, hidden completely from the watchful eyes of the guards.

Fear of what might come of him was building up inside, his heart thumped with uncertainty. Be thrown into prison or get dumped somewhere else were two possible scenarios that could happen. But he had burned bridges and left everything behind in order to fulfill the dream that he had desired to obtain.

The hold was large enough to contain many huge boxes where he could temporarily hide himself. In between these boxes and crates were spaces considerably wide for a person to fit himself although quite uncomfortably. Jonas did not show signs of unnecessary movements or any sounds that could attract the crew, and here he slept for the night.

Morning came the following day, 10th August, year 1519. It was sunny, and the dock was jam-packed with housewives, sisters, brothers, parents, girlfriends and well-wishers when the five galleons departed from the port of Seville. Overflowing with kisses and last farewells the five galleons, laden with goods and men who were sent on a unique mission to the Far East, unfurled sails and drifted majestically out into the broad sea from Guadalquivir River.

Jonas held on but not for so long. It was sweltering inside and to avoid cramps he had to stretch his muscles every now and then. When the ships were far out into the sea, he figured it was time for him to go out of hiding. He could see there was ample probability that the galleons would not go back to Seville to drop him. In all likelihood he would be deposited and left in the next port of destination, but this did not diminish the spirit that took him this far. He was shaking inside of uncertainties yet full of hopes and aspirations.

"If I had turned chicken, what would have become of my life?" he dwelt on the thought. "Life would have been different with no challenge at all. It would then be the same all day, monotonous and dragging in Seville. School was not an option anymore. I needed to have something to cling to- a once in a lifetime opportunity which would take me somewhere on my own. Neither would dependence on my parents would do me any good. But would this future in other places give me the assurance I was looking for? Not at all, I was aware of that. It was also a gamble. The stakes were high and I took it."

"*Señor Capitan*, we have two stowaways. We found them hiding among the cargoes," reported one crew member.

"I want to see them. Bring them in," ordered the captain.

"Right away, sir."

They were brought before the captain, practically dragged, Jonas and another young lad, who was also hiding with him at the hold, their eyes squinting at the sudden exposure to light. They crossed the upper deck, bumping on the railings and on the walls, stumbling with weak footings then were shoved inside through the open door.

The captain's cabin was spacious and warm. There was a map of Europe on one wall and the world on the other. Behind his desk was a shelf stacked with Atlases and tomes of nautical books. There was a coat hanger to the left of his desk and he was reading. As they were jostled inside, the captain looked up behind his spectacles.

"Jonas! How on earth. . ." evidently he was flustered to see him. He stood up and pounded his clenched fist on the table.

Jonas was mute. His eyes were locked on to the captain's who refused to blink. Out of the porthole, the rushing of the waves told him they were leagues away from land. A moment of stunned silence , then the captain opened his mouth in disbelief, "how did you...? Well... forget it. Jonas...I don't want to trouble myself of how you did it, but your mother must be worried as hell now." A trace of displeasure crossed the captain's face.

"Well, you told me there's no way you could do it. I found a way myself," Jonas was stubbornly defiant. He stared at the captain then looked away, boldly disrespectful.

To avoid seeing his insolent face the captain turned to the other lad. The severity of his voice did not change, but his expression softened upon diverting his gaze to him, "young man, what's your name?" he said authoritatively.

"Me llamo Daniel Cervantes, señor."

"¿De dónde eres?"

"Soy de Madrid, señor."

Jonas heard the questioning and the answers but his eyes were busy roaming around the cabin, scanning all the corners and the things which were neatly arranged on the desk. It confirmed his uncle's knack for absolute order. There at one corner was the oak box. Why it glowed at the seams was a puzzle that troubled his young curious mind. He was mum. He knew his present position did not warrant for him to be so aggressively inquisitive, so he immediately resigned to the fact that satisfying himself would be out of timing and could be done at a later time when all other circumstances would allow.

The Captain eyed both of the lads sharply, from one to the other then back to the other, not knowing what to do with them stowaways. He swallowed hard to regain control. He could not afford to show a sign of weakness, so to establish firm control he pronounced his decision starkly, "do you know that you will be punished for this? You will be shipped back to Spain on the next stop. Meanwhile you'll be put on hold," then he looked at the guard, "go tell Jose I want to see him, right away."

"Yes, sir."

"Boys, I surely will get back to you," he dismissed them with a wave of his hand.

The captain's control did not in any manner as much bothered Jonas at all. Everything he said was clear but never menacing. Being a nephew he was sure his uncle was only acting under his authority as the captain and would never ever decide on something that would harm him in any way. His mind was more fixed on the oak box at the corner. What was inside that could give off so much light bothered him more than his uncle's admonition.

Captain Juan Serrano sighed deeply after they left. He had high respect for Jonas' brave action, though how immature it had been, knowing that the hardships back in Seville was what led him to stow away, to get a chance of a change in a lifetime in whatever manner and ways it may be, and that change could only be attained by joining the voyage. Even in his younger days, he had noticed the obstinacy or determination in Jonas' character to obtain what he wanted so much in life- a quality which he had admired secretly. Stowing away in his galleon was nothing but a means to acquire such longing for a change and a minor offense as that. In any case, he would stand to be blamed by the family if something ever happened to Jonas without him lifting a finger to help. So assigning him in the kitchen temporarily would do him well, save him from hunger or at least tide him over from any uncertainties in this long rigorous voyage. He managed to justify his actions .

Going out into the upper deck, Jonas decided that knowing all the places, parts and nooks of this galleon, if he were to survive within its confines for months of travel was the wisest thing to do. When he stepped out into the quarterdeck, he studied the galleon's interior structure. He walked around, looked up and marveled at the four mast sails standing in the middle and the crow's nest, which was the watchman's station. He saw that this ship had three decks: the aft castle, where the captain's cabin was located; and the poop deck, which was at the topmost and formed the roof, where the steering officer navigates the ship; the forecastle, was in the lower deck where the cots were placed side by side to each other for the crews to sleep. Far ahead was the whole stretch of the upper deck up to the end where ordinary personnel stayed most of the time to work, talk and wriggle out the monotony of the voyage; In the middle of the upper deck was the capstan, where he and Daniel would be seeing each other after work. He calculated that *Santiago*, this galleon, was about a thousand tons in weight excluding its cargoes and crew members. Huge enough but he learned later that it was smaller than the other four galleons. His tour was prematurely interrupted when one of the men told him to see Jose at the kitchen.

The kitchen was narrow with two long counters at the sides: Pans and pots were strewn on one counter. Cutting boards were on the other beside the bucket of potatoes. In the middle were pans hanging from the ceiling. On the floor were two bags of flour. One was open. Above one of the counters was a porthole which opened towards the sea, through which you see the vast horizon and hear the rushing of the waves. When he entered there were two men working side by side. One greeted him. It was Jose, the chief cook.

He was stirring beef stew in a big pot then looked up. "So I heard you'll be working with us?"

"Yeah, where do I start?" he answered snappily.

He must have sounded too eager to start working that he sensed Jose putting on the brakes, "relax, young man. You'll have all the time in this world. All I want you to do as yet is to observe. This afternoon you'll start doing kitchen work already. Let me now organize myself and see what we could do."

"Thank you, Jose."

"Go around and learn what you see, ok?"Then he put the big ladle on its rack.

"Would you like me to come back when you're free?"

"Yes, enjoy yourself first."

The other lad was Luis Mendoza from Valencia. He threw Jonas a wink and said he was glad to be working with him at the kitchen.

These were the first people he met among the hotchpotch of men from different countries. He learned that majority of them were Spaniards. Some were from Italy, Portugal and France. Two men were from Morocco. Jose, he guessed was Italian judging from his accent.

He and Daniel were assigned spaces in the lower deck. It's where junior officers live. Space was extremely limited and the cots were separated from the rest by curtains. One cot was on top of another saving on precious space. Of course for the Captain and his officers the conditions were relatively comfortable. In good weather the men stayed on the upper deck where the air was fresh.

He went to the stern then walked towards the bow, looked around, but could find nothing of what he was looking for. He realized there was something missing in this galleon, he panicked.

"Where shall I pooh?" he looked for an answer somewhere.

Well, to panic was an exaggerated reaction to say the most. Back in Seville houses had no facility of comfort whatsoever, and people were used to other means of disposals.

Jonas looked far ahead where the undiscovered horizon loomed, contemplating as to what was forthcoming. So many stories abound as to the end of the sea. "Is it the limit? If it was then would we fall down on reaching it, swallowed into the bottom of the black ocean?" he reflected. On another perspective there were also stories about conquered territories, booties and gold beyond anybody's imagination. "Where ever the voyage would take me doesn't matter anymore. All the challenges and obstacles I would be facing seemed smaller now that I'm here. I am already in the water, so I might as well swim in it, follow the tide and make the most of everything," he mused with renewed vitality and excitement.

CHAPTER 28

Predictably the sea was calm and gentle. Waves crushed on the sides of the boat forming thin frayed bands of luminescent foam as they paddled along. Surfs which rolled past rushed to shore. It was exhilarating to watch them but the scorching sun in high noon, creating mirage images on the water, was draining.

Anywhere she went , the entourage of four ever reliable escorts Ilang-ilang's father assigned to her, two able bodied men who were also the boat rowers and two young reliable maids at her service, were always at her side. Her safety had not been left to chance by the Datu. She had grown to be a pretty young lady so that a security cordon around her was seen necessary wherever she went. Their great-grandmas' abduction still lingered in their minds, a precedent that reinforced his over-protectiveness on his only daughter. What with all the men in Sugbo and Opon who were interested in her?

Her grandma's hut was up in the hills with a good view of the whole village. It was fenced around with short bushes and tall mango trees which added coolness, which made it well covered from the afternoon sun. To visit her was tedious and long yet this did not mar Ilang-ilang's love to see her as often as she could. After crossing the channel for about an hour, the land trip, and the visit to the shops they stopped-over her cousin's place in Sugbo, daughters of the Rajah to take a rest before proceeding to the hills. Dayang and Dana, the eternally dependable sisters, of her age and fun to be with, were always accommodating and honest to themselves. They always made her comfortable.

"How's the trip, cousin?" inquired Dayang.

"If they only put up something to connect these two islands, it would have been an easy trip. Crossing the channel every time I come is too exhausting," Ilang-ilang commented.

"Do you mean a bridge?" confirmed Dayang of Ilang-ilang's remark. She lifted a jug and willingly served cool fresh coco milk to her.

Ilang-ilang reached for the glass and took a sip, "Thank you, cousin. This is refreshing."

After a short swig Ilang-ilang continued, "Yeah, sort of, where one could easily cross on foot."

"That's a nice idea but I can see no possibilities for it to happen in a short period of time considering the distance. It's too far and wide. That would require years of professional work and a lot of material to use," Dana who was sitting at the corner of the salon joined in.

Resigned to the idea Ilang-ilang parried Dana's comment, "I guess I would have to make do with the boat."

"Hm... Perhaps in a hundred years that would become a possibility," continued Dana looking at her with cynical empathy.

"Take a rest before you go to grandma's," offered Dayang.

"Thanks, cousin, but I still have to do some bartering at the market. I could grab a nap at grandmas afterward." She put her bag aside and crossed the salon towards the window to check if the weather was still cooperating.

Dayang was the older of the two, more mature and caring. Dana was two years younger, prettier, and candid in her remarks. Young daughters of the Rajah, who did nothing but made themselves prettier in make-ups and new dresses.

"If only grandma would live with us."

"Well, you know her reasons. Your frequent visits to her would not change anything," Dayang served a glassful of the coco milk for Dana.

Ilang-ilang paced to and fro near the window then stated, "I love seeing her and if it needs me to cross the channel every time, then I would do it for nothing in this world."

"Why don't you sleep here for the night, cousin?" offered Dayang.

"Yeah, why not," seconded Dana.

"I will but some other time, perhaps. Besides I don't have permission from home to sleep over. You know how *Tata* would feel."

"He's so unfair. As if he were free of any wrongdoings. When it's you he' so damn strict you couldn't move around. Look, men can't even approach you, too intimidated at the sight of your four escorts – a double standard mentality when it comes to you, cousin," commented Dana.

"Yeah, cousin, It didn't occur to me that they would keep men away," seconded Dayang.
Ilang-ilang changed the topic abruptly, as if this alone would cover up for her father's over protectiveness and concern for her, by taking out a dress she recently got from one of the shops and showed it to them.

"What do you think of this dress?"

"It's nice and specially sensuous. You would look lovely with this," complimented Dayang, inspecting the dress by turning it over and over on either sides, then handed it back to her. How much did you get it for?"

"A basket and a half of eggs. I think it was a good barter considering its quality and uniqueness of style." Dayang and Dana made no comments knowing that Ilang-ilang was a better dresser than both of them.

She put the dress back into the bag and placed it on top of the table then slumped herself onto the sofa, and an idea came to her mind.

"Why don't you come with me to Opon so that we could go swimming? The sea is quite inviting these days," she offered.

"That's a good idea," Dayang exclaimed, eyes widened.

"We'll have barbecued fish and shrimps. I'll ask Yaya Nabilah to prepare everything for us."

"Let's set it for next Saturday, cousin," Dana's voice raised a little with excitement at the prospect of going on a beach picnic.

"Do you want me to pick you up?" Ilang-ilang offered honestly.

"Don't bother, cousin. We could manage," said Dayang.

"Ok then, if the sky is clear."

Her visits to Sugbo and to her grandma would not have been made possible if it were not for the valuable services of her four ever reliable escorts, whose respective roles made her movements possible and easy. She recognized this and was ever thankful to their services, rowing her boat and attending to her needs. However, she felt to a certain degree that her movements were indeed unnecessarily restrained. She had some misgivings, albeit she could go wherever she wanted to, when young men of her age were in fact held-off by their presence.

Her two cousins were undeniably right. She was overly protected and the dangers she had been covered from were merely imaginary. This began to slowly revolt her senses so much. Yet she hasn't shown any revulsions towards her father whom she respected and loved dearly.

CHAPTER 29

It was towards the end of summer when the five galleons slid majestically towards the African coast. Looking up, Jonas saw swallows in v-shape migrating to the equator obviously to find food and be away from the cold. Ahead of them were the four resplendent galleons moving forward in equal cadence. Since then he had reasons to believe that they made their course towards Cape Verde, by passing Tenerife and some islands. He felt his heart slowed a bit at the thought that they would drop them in Tenerife. However this did not happen when they passed some islands and the Cape. Having reached as far as this, the commander set their course in the direction of Brazil by crossing the great Atlantic Ocean towards the southwest. The voyage was long and monotonous it took them four months to see the contours of a great mass of land later he learned was America.

"Check," Luis calculated, after moving his queen on the board in front of Jonas.

"I have to get away from your queen or I'll be stuck, pawn to move."

"Check from my tower. I think you're mate, Jonas."

Luis was the champion in their galleon. Nobody had ever beaten him in this game. But Jonas was learning. He said he should concentrate on the center and never take the queen out early in the game. His advice, though, never taught Jonas how to play the game so well to beat him.

Jonas' made friends with everybody, which gesture gave him a circle of security, honestly showing concern to all their needs. He knew he would be with them for the entire voyage, and being nice was the best thing that he could do to alleviate the monotony.

"Land . . . long stretch of land, *señor*," hollered the watchman at the crow's nest, pointing at the high mountains far away.

Brazil was a long stretch of land facing the treacherous Atlantic Ocean. The surrounding waters were cold, uninviting deep green, with the freezing currents encircling continuously. Thankfully the continent itself was an sanctuary of Brazil woods, wide marshes, meadows and green forest teeming with wild animals and birds. They had also run out of drinking water, so here they saw the opportunity to fill all their containers before resuming with the journey.

"Head twenty three degrees south latitude. Let's stay along the coast," instructed the commander.

They reached as far as Cape Frio.

"Then from there, steer to the west for about thirty leagues," he ordered expecting to see an opening to the west. But they ended up in Rio de Janeiro.

After five months, they entered the port of Rio de Janeiro and stayed there until Christmas day. The voyage priest conducted masses on the quarterdeck then they had a little celebration of singing, with wine and roast lamb and turkey. They hauled in drinking water and some provisions. After celebrating Christmas they took up sailing again, the following day.

"We go southward and follow the shoreline," ordered the Commander.

"*Señor*, on the left is a town. Shall we embark?" announced the second mate.

"No, go on. Let's see if we could find a way out to the other side."

The town was Liha Grande.

The Commander ordered the course down south, thinking they would find a way, but they found out that they got into a huge gulf for which they stayed for two months. They steered from this gulf, cruising along the coast, further on to the south where they discovered a point, to which they gave the name Point of San Sebastian. Then they ran to the southwest, and entered a channel which was named Lihabela. Thenceforth they took the passage to the southwest to some shoals, which they named Shoals of the Currents, because the currents were strong in spite of the shallow waters.

Monotony was a killer. For the past six months life had been full of routines, Jonas could swear to the mermaids in the ocean that it had been so bad. Same work, same people and the same conversations and no variations. Everybody felt trapped and so was he.

What's monotony anyway? It's plainly a set of meaningless routines, boring and unfulfilling. It was time to fight back, do something to kill monotony, to think of some practical useful things to do. He thought of reading, but he had run out of reading materials. Going into arts and did some wood carvings was an option. Working was another.

"The water's ready," Jonas told Jose.

The process was tediously long. He had to fetch water from the sea until the bucket was full. Then heated the water, put in some soap and stirred the solution, careful not to waste any drop. Everything gets used, recycled, stored and used again until the water gets murky. He glanced at Jose before testing the temperature of the water with his finger. He used this for cleaning the kitchen.

At the same time he was doing something else. "So what should I do with the broth?" Jonas looked at him, tasting a bit of it on a wooden ladle.

"Put a handful of salt in it and stir."

After tasting the broth, he put the ladle down then washed the pots and pans at the sides without saying anything. The remaining water in the bucket, he used to mop the floor.

Daniel and Jonas became to know each other more. They developed an extraordinary kind of friendship which was built on necessity. When they were free from work they were always together at the capstan talking, trying to learn something and sharing secrets. Jonas learned that both of them had something in common and had the same ambitions and aspirations in life. Daniel confided that he had studied Medicine in Madrid but left school without finishing when family finances went tight. Daniel had dreamed of travelling and seeing distant places, too. This led him to go to Seville drawn by the prospect of good life. He was likewise one of those rejected by the enlistment. They were found on the upper deck, sitting on the capstan. Daniel stretched his leg and looked at him. Jonas was busy peeling a bucket of potatoes.

"How's your assignment at the kitchen?"

"To tell you the truth, I can't complain…so far so good. Jose is kind enough to teach me the things I need to know such as the right amount of ingredients enough to serve sixty men."

"I'm glad you're doing fine. Now that we are here, Jonas, I would like your honest opinion. Are we going to be sent back or thrown to prison?"

"I'm sorry I can tell you nothing, Daniel. It's been my desire to stay and continue the voyage until the end. So far, I haven't heard anything of the sort."

"To tell you frankly, I'm afraid."

"My heart slowed down when we passed Tenerife and the Canary Islands; I was praying we would never stop. Now we're here too far away to go back. We'll cross fingers and hope for the best."

"I heard our sleeping spaces would be for keeps."

"Yeah . . we hang on, behave well and see what the boss would say. I heard that two of the enlisted men failed to come at the departure. That's why they gave us the spaces. One was sickly bedridden and the other died in an accident."

"So that's why . . . now, I understand. We were lucky he was your uncle, Jonas. Otherwise we would have been thrown overboard. Is he honestly your uncle?" Jonas was silent. His mind was far away, contemplating.

"Do you have any ideas where we are heading?" Daniel was interested in knowing.

"Well . . . I heard we're looking for territories and a way to the east. They wanted to explore this way to prove that the earth does not end at the horizon, and to find an island which was the source of some wealth, perhaps gold and silver. Only the commander knows where they are. They say, towards the Far East. I supposed we're going that way. The Captain Commander believes that he could find an opening to the other side. He is trying this route, everything is new."

"And?" he responded laconically.

"Yes, in fact some people have been there already, through the other route. The Commander who's a Portuguese himself had known the existence of these islands. So he went to Spain to convince the King to finance him this trip because nobody in Portugal had believed he could do it the other way."

"How did you know all of this?"

"I always listen to older folks talk about this and that." Jonas was always curious. He wanted to learn the reasons for anything unusual or strange- a trait which had broadened his horizons and sometimes got him into trouble.

This curiosity troubled him every night when it was time for bed. He was uneasy, beset by the same trivial imaginations of the box, his other self urging him to go into the captain's cabin and see for himself the contents, once and for all, which now got stronger and stronger. His curious self was telling him to do it, and see why it glowed at the seams. "Or was it only my imagination which was playing tricks on me? But I wanted some explanations," he pondered. "How would I do it without being caught? Would I just go and ask my uncle directly? This would make things simpler. Would I tell Daniel? I decided not until I got it opened and saw its contents."

The day was long and tiring so they thought it was time for them to separate ways and go down to the lower deck for their respective cots to rest.

"Good night, Jonas."

"See you tomorrow, friend."

Daniel yawned got down from the capstan then headed towards his designated resting place. Jonas did the same.

"It was comforting to be in my little cubicle, peaceful in solitude to meditate in my own time. I opened my Bible and read a verse about Jonah who was swallowed by a big fish. And because of his undying belief and prayer God commanded the fish to vomit him onto dry land, after three days and three nights inside its stomach. I loved reading it, not only in the similarity of our names but also in the absurdity of his plight inside this big fish exemplified by the mind boggling infinite power of God," Jonas contemplated.

You hurled me into the deep, into the very heart of the seas, and the currents swirled about me; all your waves and breakers swept over me . . . The engulfing waters threatened me, the deep surrounded me; seaweed was wrapped around my head. To the roots of the mountains I sank down; the earth beneath barred me in forever. But you brought my life up from the pit.
"O Lord God, Bless my soul."

This was how he got out from the rut: to pray and talked to somebody who was more powerful than anybody else. Then he put the Bible under his pillow, closed his eyes and drifted off to sleep.

CHAPTER 30

It was a clear day, noontime, when the sun was up and the road was steaming hot towards the hills where Ilang-ilang's grandma had her little abode. Not a soul in the streets of Sugbo was up and about. Up in the hills the air was cooler and steaming hot tea was about to be served on her grandma's table.

She poured a cup skillfully and handed it over to Ilang-ilang. Her voice hoarse, "here you are, my dear child."

Ilang-ilang daintily reached out and took a little sip. Her beauty sparkled where ever she was and her answers were always respectful, "thanks *Nenek*."

"Was your trip here easy?"

"Yes, it was, but the heat of the road was unbearable."

"Well, tell me about what's going on now in Opon." Her grandma pulled a stool from under the table and lowered herself slowly onto it.

"Nothing much, but *Nana* and *Tata* were again at odds with you living separately far away from us. She wants you to stay with us but he insisted on respecting your independence."

"There's always that eternal conflict. I would say that your *Nana* is thoughtful. And I admire her for being so," she grunted.

"As always, she has been after your welfare and well-being, *Nenek*," Ilang-ilang said gently, a thoughtful look printed on her lovely face.

Then grandma crossed her legs. "I know my dear child, but I'd prefer to live here on my own."

"Haven't you forgiven *Tata* for what he had done, *Nenek*?" a concerned voice came out from within.

Grandma shook her head. "Forgiveness is a two edge sword, child. The other side is the good one. If I took it, I would then be living with you, see you every day and share with you everything, in all the remaining happy moments of my life. The other side would kill me, so I'd rather be away from your *Tata* than see him every day and eat myself out with anger. I have already forgiven him long time ago, but I cannot live with him anymore."

"But forgiving is forgetting you were hurt, *Nenek*," Ilang-ilang earnestly persuaded her. As always her efforts failed in the process.

"Yes, you are right, my child. But after fighting with your grandpa and taking his life, it's as if he snatched away a part of me, too. And that part had been buried along with your grandpa. It's only your great-grandma Hana in the family who had forgotten completely, but it would be too difficult for me to forget."

She poured herself little tea barely enough to fill her cup and took a sip, observing her grandma carefully, "this is the grandma I've seen all my life and loved all my life." As she pondered, a feeling of pity ran through her, "over the years her anger with *Tata* reflected on her face and she looked older than Lala Hana. I know that her life was hard and frequently painful living alone by herself. Yet I am also aware that this was often cushioned by her good sense of humor and a great surviving spirit. Not surprisingly enough she has reached eighty three."

As her grandma continued to watch Ilang-ilang, a glimmer of moisture appeared in her eyes. Then she changed the course of conversation.

"Oh, by the way, thank you for the mangoes, my dear child." She got one from the basket and brought it close to her nose to smell it. "They're ripe for eating," she commented honestly. She pulled a knife from a cupboard then cut the mango in three parts.

"You're welcome, *Nenek*. Why don't we go to Sandakan and visit, great-grandma Hana?" Ilang-ilang took out a small plate and gave it to her grandma.

Her grandma reached for it with her left hand and placed the mango on top , then offered it to Ilang-ilang. "That has been part of my plans for the future, my dear, but I still want to be near your mother. I believe that she still needs me. Here in Sugbo, it's nearer and she could come and visit anytime she wishes to see me."

"Well, you were in Sandakan when great grandpa Amir was buried. If I had the chance I would go and visit Lala Hana."

"That was five years ago my dear child. I miss your Lala Hana already. If it were not for the boat trips I would have been there again. I can't take them anymore. They're too long and the sea . . . I have some fears of the dark sea, my child." She smirked at the thought.

A chord of compassion ran through Ilang-ilang's whole being. It rose in perfect harmony to her grandma's sufferings, giving credence to her grandfather's untimely death, and the immutability of it all on her father's culpability. A knit of contradictory consciousness within the family which was difficult to untangle.

"Please lead me to where grandpa is, *Nenek*," requested Ilang-ilang courteously. She took her grandma's hand, stepped out of the hut ,then went behind it. They stood in front of a mound where he had been laid to rest. She put down the flowers she brought on top and made some prayers.

"He would still have been alive if he had listened to me. Fighting with your *Tata* was the craziest thing he had ever done. Your Tata was younger and stronger." Pain was in her eyes and she looked at her granddaughter with empathy.

"I'm sorry about that, *Nenek*. But let's talk about how you're getting along, alone in this hut,"

Her grandma continued without giving heed to her cutting remark, repetitiously recalling everything that had happened in the past.

"Your grandpa was a good man. He would still have lived if he had not been so tenacious against their relationship. It cost his life trying to break them up. Your *nana* was hard-headed. We always told her to keep away from him, but they always saw each other behind our backs. On that tragic day, when grandpa caught them at the river, he was unable to control his anger and fought with him. Your *Tata* did not want to fight but it was too late. He was younger and stronger," she shrugged.

"Anyway, if it didn't happen I wouldn't have been here with you, grandma."

"So they eloped and lived in Sugbo, leaving all of us in Sandakan dumbstruck at the tragedy. I followed afterwards. I tried to live with them but there was always a conflict. So here I am now living alone at the top of this hill."

Ilang-ilang had to repeat her words , "I wouldn't have been born if not for what happened, so everything took their places normally as they were."

The air was getting colder then she decided to get back inside. While taking the walk back to the hut, one small detail occurred to Ilang-ilang, "I want some clarifications, *Nenek*. Grandpa died in Sandakan and what you have here buried were his ashes, right?"

"I had been carrying his ashes anywhere I go, dear child. I decided to bury them here where I believed I would live for the rest of my life."

"I'm aware of that through *Nana*, grandma. You know there's an extra room at home for you. If you're tired of living alone here, the house is open for you. *Nana* and I would love to have you home."

"Thank you again, my sweet child."

Her grandma was emotional. As soon as they were inside she took a seat beside the window. They shifted to silent mood. It was a prolonged silence after which she stood up, went to her bed and took out the velvet bag from its hiding place. The pearls had been once her pride. She found constant pleasure in them, but now in her last remaining years she had to part with them, so that they would end up in one of her grandchildren's possession.

"My dear Ilang-ilang, I'm getting old and they have been with me for years. Take them. I'd love to see them with you." Grandma handed her the velvet bag. "Please do take care of them. I know they would bring you good luck."

"These are the pearls from great-grandma Hana?"

"They're yours. You are the rightful owner now."

"Thank you, *Nenek*. But how about *Nana*?"

"Sh." She stopped her from saying anything.

But Ilang-ilang continued, surprised at the decision to bypass her mother. "...tradition says that it should be *Nana* who should take them after you."

Her grandma didn't say anything for a brief moment, and then let out a deep breath. She could see pain in her eyes. "Your *nana* has lost the hierarchy of the legacy. It went with your grandpa's death. Time will justify my reasons, my dear child. They are yours. You need them more than I do now that you have grown up to be a young lady. Only remember that when problems set in you could always rely on them pearls. They have helped your ancestors for as long as I could remember, so there would be no reasons why they would not do likewise to you or bring you fortunes in the future."

CHAPTER 31

Months of sea travel was getting rough and slow. Monotony seeped into everybody's mood, which occasionally got some into a fight at the slightest provocation. At the corner, seated on huge anchor cables men played chess, cards, read books or chat. Some did nothing but stared emptily at the horizon. Occupying themselves in some useful activities was the soothing balm, the remedy or they fell into doing something foolish. Work was the best time killer, the best deviation of the mind but it also became drudgery as they worked aimlessly.

They were in the vast ocean for months without seeing land, only miles and miles of water and the sky, it was discouraging for the weak-of-hearts . Supply of drinking water was low they had to pray for rain to come. Fruits and vegetables also ran out. All they had left was preserved food and it was strictly controlled. Hunger made stomachs grumble and tempers ran short.

Jonas boiled soup, mopped floors and did some errands in the kitchen without complaining. His assignment was tedious but he was thankful because of the privilege of being near to food and never going hungry. He always cared for his friend and shared this privilege with him by preparing some food when nobody was around at the kitchen.

In his free time, he never failed to see his friend. He was always careful nobody knew about this charity he was doing. He looked around to see if somebody was snooping, took out a sandwich from his pocket and slipped it secretly to him.

"Here, I prepared a *bocadillo* for you. But be discreet, 'cause nobody knows," he advised his friend.

"*Gracias*," Daniel was ever grateful at his friend's thoughtfulness.

"No problem."

The whole mission now needed more doctors and assistance from those who had some medical knowledge. Daniel Cervantes was soon assigned to assist the medical team on knowing his medical background. Going rounds with the doctor and assisting him to see who got cough and colds or fever, was his routine. He had to jump from ship to ship, especially if the cases were serious such as surgeries and amputations.

"There's so much work to do now that almost everybody's got high temperatures. There's one who chilled the whole night and did not make it, he succumbed to the plague," confided Daniel.

Then he continued, sighing deeply , "I'm afraid more men wouldn't be able to make it. Worse is that we're running out of medicines."

"Is there a solution to that?" Jonas asked.

"Being careful not to get it from others."

"You are in close contact with the sick. You should be careful you don't get it yourself," Jonas cautioned Daniel, which reminded him of his mother's favorite phrase.

"Well, the doctor gave us some precautions, thank God. One thing was to advise people to cover their mouths when they sneeze so that they wouldn't spread the virus."

"But there's still the risk you get it through touch and sight, right?"

"That's the risk in attending them. So far I have been lucky."

"Why is it that some don't get it?" Jonas was curious.

"It's because they are immune."

"What is that?"

"When you had been downed with the sickness before, you won't get it for the second time, your body gets used to it, and your defenses get stronger."

"I see . . . similar to measles? Once you had it you won't get it for the second time."

"Yeah . . ."

"Many men are sick now because it's a new strain, said the doctor. There are some lucky ones who don't get it because their bodies are stronger."

"I think it's the food we are eating. It's unbalanced. Our body badly needs vitamins we only get from green vegetables and fresh fruits. All we have is preserved food in jars, morning till night."

"Well, what's wrong with preserved food?"

"Still they're not enough. We need vegetables and fruits, as I have said. Then there's the issue of hygiene. If only men clean their cots and wash their clothes, we would prevent virus and bacteria to germinate and spread," added Daniel.

At night the galleons echoed with the sound of sneezing, retching, wheezing and coughing which signaled the outbreak of illnesses. It penetrated the cots and the dividing curtains which filled them with dread. Spaces were miserable. They were sleeping on top of one another they heard noises of disease, and getting sick was getting more real. Scurvy found itself among the weak, their skin peeled, bled and pussy. It often represented itself initially with symptoms of depression and weariness then advanced to death.

That night Jonas was getting restless. He heard men coughing and sneezing and feared that he would get it. He tossed and shifted positions then pulled the blanket over his face. "Tomorrow would be another beginning, another struggle, another misery," he shuddered, worried with the thought.

One fifth of the original number of men who joined in this journey perished because of deteriorating health and their number was dwindling every day. Bodies were wrapped with their blankets then thrown into the waters . Many more were sick and were holding out.

CHAPTER 32

Sugbo had been a thriving port at the center of several smaller islands. Imports from the neighboring islands ended up in its market and goods from different places came to be traded every day filling all the shops everywhere. Growth was the inevitable course. The obvious reason for its steady growth and progress was attributed to its ideal strategic geographical location. Sugbo was safely surrounded by mountainous islands that shielded it from strong storms and typhoons. Exactly opposite from the village was Opon Island which fortified it even more from any strong winds, for which reason confidence from traders rose evidently. Even ships that found themselves in the middle of storms found refuge in its safe bosom.

The downside was that once beautiful beaches now had been transformed into docking places for commercial ships turning the coastline inaccessible to local bathers, and converting the village the hub and center of all the unavoidable activities for which they had been created- a price the villagers had to pay for progress.

Better life and easy access to goods compensated for all the changes that had happened. Markets abound in food and clothing, fresh and new from their sources. Food was never lacking and everybody had gainful occupations. Stalls bartering from bags, dresses, sarongs, and the necessary adornments for young women glittered in their display. Baskets, pots, pans, utensils, vases littered the streets for sale. The only capacity for one to obtain them was to have goods of equal value to barter with, in the absence of currencies.

Sugbo was a typically Asian monarchial society with the Rajah as the head. His powers were comprehensive and wide-ranging and normally without any controls from any branch of the territory. Under him were Datus who ruled smaller principalities within the territory called *barangays*, like Ilang-ilang's father who was responsible for the island of Opon. The minions, called *Olipons*, were the lesser members of society who normally contributed labor and goods from their produce, as a tribute to their heads of state.

Migration of people from all over increased. Still land was available up north. Beyond the village were sprawling acres and acres of mountainous domains still virgin and ideal for palatial residential houses. At the foot of these higher lands were hills overlooking the entirety of Sugbo, perched as such with the breathtaking view of the whole village, its rooftops, the sea that separates it with Opon and its skyline that would bring your imaginations to greater heights, especially over at the horizon where you wondered at the magic of the early morning sun by the time it starts to spread its golden rays over the land.

Sugboanons were familiar with foreigners for they had interacted with them for centuries. They had seen other travelers from as far as China, Borneo and Malaysia, for which contact the opportunity to cultivate friendly relationships with them flourished steadily. In fact the native Sugboanon is an amalgam of so many races from these places, what with years and years of inter marriages and interaction among the different peoples. They were never ignorant of their visits, and their presence had almost become a common integral occurrence in their lives.

In spite of these interactions, a native Sugboanon was still wary of trade invasions from other faraway lands they had never ever heard before. Nobody ever forgot the invasions from the north, killing so many of their brothers and burning their homes to the ground. The memory was imprinted still fresh in their minds giving them reasons to be cautious, sometimes xenophobic, which had never been eradicated in their closed ethnic mentality.

CHAPTER 33

A new day came and the two friends saw each other again at the capstan. They talked about all the miseries they had seen around and the number of bodies thrown overboard. Poor wretched men, with love ones who were expecting to see them back home. Men who were unfortunate enough to have lost their lives without seeing the closing stages of their journey.

"Hey, I see you had your hair cut?"

"I used a knife to do it, with a mirror. You know I don't trust the barber anymore. He uses the same comb and scissors for everybody without washing before using them for the next one. It's one way to transmit one's illness." Daniel tipped his head left and right to show him how he looked.

"I think you did an exceptionally good job with it. That gives me an idea: you cut mine and I cut yours next time."

"I think that's one way from getting sick, Jonas. Half of this sandwich I will keep for tomorrow. Thanks again."

"Don't mention it."

When they parted Daniel never stopped thinking about the men who lost their lives, some of them his friends, unnecessarily taken away by a stroke of fate. If only there was a way to control the spread of disease, he pondered deeply.

On the other hand, Jonas' mind lingered and never got off from thinking about the mysterious box. He decided that in one of these days, he would slip into the captain's cabin, open it and finally end his agony. A screwdriver or a knife could come in handy. After opening it, and have satisfied his curiosity he would have to close it back in a manner that nobody would notice. Why did it glow? He kept searching for a logical answer.

Perched on this thought, he saw a black rat darting towards the hold where the provisions were kept. He followed its way until he saw it with three others nibbling at the sack of rice. There must be more of them here, he smirked at the thought. He went straight to Jose to report what he saw.

Jose was elderly at about thirty five, who wore a pair of glasses he seemed to be more of a professor at the university than being a chief cook at the galleon. He was lying on his cot with a blanket over him.

Jonas sat down on the edge of his cot. "You're shivering Jose. Can I help?"

"This is nothing, Jonas. Only a little fever. Could you please reach out for the jug of water?"

"Here you are," Jonas tipped the jug to make it easier for him to wet his dry lips.

Jose took a sip and put the jug down beside him on the floor, then moved his hips to make himself comfortable.

"Thank you. Why are you here?" he queried with a weak voice.

"To see how you're doing. I saw how pale you were at the kitchen; I guessed something was wrong with you. I hope your fever would go down soon. Would you like me to do something for you?" Jonas lied.

The chief cook replied no more. He shifted again and turned around. Jonas decided the issue about the rat could be raised some other time when he was ready to talk about it. Jose pulled and straightened his blanket then Jonas left him half asleep shivering.

With all of them crammed in small spaces, sanitation was also a major problem. A lack of proper toilet facilities meant that they used something else. Jonas soon felt uncomfortable doing it at the bilge, where the sea water and waste were collected. Then buckets were used to throw the waste into the sea. When Jonas went to the bilge he had to stop breathing because it stunk of waste and urine. This was how depressing the situation was, but were there any alternatives?

The following morning Jonas saw Jose at the kitchen. He was now feeling fine. The fever had gone down and his appetite improved. He told him to take a rest.

"Hey, Jonas, I want you to make inventories of the stocks we have." Still weak from his fever, he moved weakly at the side of the table and balanced himself.

Jonas moved swiftly to offer for help, but Jose insisted in doing it alone by holding the table firmly. "Is it necessary, Jose?" Then he grabbed a chair for him to sit. Jose staggered feebly and dropped down on the chair.
"I don't want to accuse anybody, but our supply of wheat and grain has gone down so fast." Jose sighed.

"I don't think any of our men are doing that. What will they do with them? How will they bake the bread or cook the rice without anybody knowing it?"

"What are you implying?" Jose's eyebrows furrowed.

"Rats . . . I've seen them with my own eyes, Jose. So many of them now are at the hold where we keep our supplies. Remember the other day we threw a sack of infested flour?"

"Yeah, I've seen some too, but I never thought they were depleting our supplies. Where do they come from?"

"I'm also wondering where they come from, they merely multiplied so fast. And I hope something is to be done with them or they'll compete with the little food we have left at the hold."

"Ok . . . I will have to make a report on this to the captain. For the meantime , could you and Luis take care of lunch?"

"That won't be a problem, Jose. Go on."

CHAPTER 34

The beach in Opon was carpeted with white sands that twinkled under the sun. It was empty with souls and the girls had the place all by themselves only. Although it was blistering farther inland, here it was merely pleasantly warm, with occasional breeze coming from the deep ocean. Atop a hillock, coconut trees swayed to the tune of the breeze. It was a bit of a remote area from Ilang-ilang's home, a walking distance that could stretch muscles before immersing into the refreshing cool water.

"I love it here, I could do it every day," exclaimed Dana, wading into the clear warm water.

"Then come every day, Dana," Ilang-ilang remarked. Then she laid the large towel on the white sand and with a graceful flow of her body lolled down beside Dayang.

"If we only have this beach in Sugbo, I would surely come every day. We have one but it's stuffed with so many bathers we could breathe no more," commented Dayang.

"The water is sparklingly clear, too," tiptoed Dayang barefooted towards the water. She looked quite sexy in her one-piece bathing suit. She got into the water wading, and then paddled herself into the deeper side. She called Ilang-ilang to join her.

Dana looked up and pointed at the sky. "Look!" High above, on wide spanned pinions, two seagulls swept above the waters to scoop swarming fish. Then they soared over the sparkling beach and veered across the sky.

"This island is blessed with so many beauties. Go around and you see miles and miles of white sand beaches. I wish it would remain virgin for more years and years to come," said Ilang-ilang.

"Talking of virginity, I noticed no special man is in sight yet, Ilang-ilang?" bantered Dana from out of the blue.

A little prick in the ego was what Ilang-ilang needed to be awakened, then she answered back sheepishly, "No, Dana. I think I would never have one if I stayed in Opon for the rest of my life. This island is beautiful but it's so bucolic."

"Well, you're still young and pretty. Dayang has one already and I think he's in love with her."

"Are you serious? Tell me who he is, Dayang."

"He is one of the young men in the village, our age. Nice guy and definitely so attentive to Dayang," volunteered Dana.

"You know, going into a relationship with someone is one thing you never think at all. If it's time for you, the right person would simply come along." Ilang-ilang looked far away and realized that her promise to lala Hana would perhaps be postponed if not broken.

"Love is another thing. And you have to work hard in order to obtain it," cut in Dayang with a voice that suggested experience.

"If what you meant is having admirers, then we don't run out of it, Dana, but my heart has ticked to no one as yet. If the right one comes along, I think my heart would tell me so. Think of the lotus which comes to life at the rising of the sun. I would open up whenever my sun comes along!" Ilang-ilang realized later that she was becoming overly defensive and repented.

"Come frequently to Sugbo and you'll meet more men of your liking," offered Dayang softly.

"I do visit you frequently."

"But when you come to Sugbo you go directly to the hills."

"Next time perhaps, I would stay longer. And that's a promise."

Their girlish chitchat was precipitately interrupted when Nabilah and Asma appeared timely with a basket of surprises. "There you are," said Asma.

"Yaya Nabilah!!," exclaimed Dana, " you have come on time. We're already famished."

"Well, what do we have here? Lobsters, crabs and shrimps!!" exclaimed Dayang.

"Yes, and all we need is a little fire," ordered Nabilah to the attending escorts, who were also enjoying among themselves at a reasonable distance, talking.

Ilang-ilang's escorts moved snappily to produce the needed fire and before long, Nabilah's fresh crawling sea creatures were already crackling and simmering on top. They ate lavishly and contentedly with their hands.

CHAPTER 35

Daniel and Jonas went to the upper deck to watch the horizon early one morning. At the distance they saw the galleons entering a large body of water, running into it thinking that there was an outlet to the east. When night came they realized it was a bay. Jonas remembered Daniel saying they were going round and round lost in a maze like a rat looking for a hole to go through, but got snagged on dead ends. He was right, Jonas affirmed him. They named this bay St. Mathew. From this bay, the days were dreary until they reached another larger one, where they caught many birds and fish.

Jonas made bread. This was one of the things the chief cook taught him: to put in the exact ingredients, mix the whole thing, knead, and flatten the dough on the table by using the heels of his palm. He kindled the oven, put the dough on a tray and chucked it inside with a wooden shovel. This had become a daily exercise, until his bread was perfect.

After his rounds with the sick, Daniel went to the capstan to take a rest. Jonas was already sitting, testing the slingshot that he had finished making.

"You got flour on your hair," he said.

"Yeah, I baked a whole lot of bread today." He dusted the flour off his hair with the left hand and took out something from his pocket with the right then gave it to Daniel.

"Here's your *bocata de jamon*."

"*Gracias*, Jonas . . . you're so kind."

"You're welcome."

" Slingshot! That would come in handy."

" . . . against rats."

"Yeah! I've seen them everywhere."

"They are everywhere at the hold where we keep our provisions. I'm worried they might contaminate the supplies, and then we'd all be sick. Maybe you have heard of the bubonic plague in Venice?"

"Yes, I have. Who hasn't?"

A moment of silence then he changed topic.

"Hey, I was wondering. What makes food go rancid?" Jonas inquired.

"When they come in contact with the air we breathe."

"So that is why we put them in big jars and cover them tightly."

"Precisely, even grain stored in this way can remain edible for five years. It's the oxygen that destroys food."

"That reminds me of my mother who used another way to preserve food. She dried meat under the sun to take out the water. She used to do it with beef. At the kitchen Jose had another way. He taught me to use salt and vinegar, and then we put them in tightly covered containers …and how about rats?"

"Of course they contaminate food. Their feces could cause blindness. Even, we, humans can destroy food by carelessness. In the kitchen, handling of food is primary or you'll poison everybody in the ship."

The conversation sunk into the mind of Jonas, and then trailed off to another direction.

"How did the Commander know about this island?" inquired Daniel.

"Well . . . the commander has a guide who is a native of one of those islands," answered Jonas as if he knew it firsthand.

"So, somebody must have been there already. We are not the first."

"Not towards the south, passing the Mediterranean sea."

"Is he here?"

"I think he is with the Commander, in the flagship."

"He must have valued him so much."

"Without a guide? I could only imagine the difficulties we would be facing. In the first place, the commander would not have been bold enough to embark in this voyage without this guide."

CHAPTER 36

The bottom of the sea was pitch dark, deep and as black as ebony. Life abound but who knew what they were like? Without meaning. On the surface, it reeked of salt and seaweeds which filled senses on crossing the channel- a poignant sensation which demonstrated life's meaningless contrasts, verdant at the surface but full of enigmas within, which invariably lead to two divergent emotions of love and indifference.

"How's your grandma, Ilang-ilang?" questioned *nana* as soon as she arrived from Sugbo.

"As always, her favorite topic is you. She always talks about you and *Tata* and how grandpa died. She keeps on repeating these things and only remembers those which hurt her so much," Ilang-ilang laid her bag down on the table and slumped on the sofa of exhaustion.

Then *nana* sat beside her to talk, "How can I force her to live with us? Her loss of memory comes with age. I'm afraid time will come she would lose her memory and wouldn't recognize us anymore."

"I always tell her to move but she's too obstinate, each time making excuses."

"It's your *Tata*."

"I know, but living alone in that small place? I'm terribly worried about her, *nana*."

"I might come with you next Sunday and force her to come."

"*Tata* might not like that. I'm disgusted, frankly disgusted, *nana*."

"Don't say that!" her nana was stunned by such impertinence.

"Neither with you nor *Tata*, but with how heaven comes down on us," Ilang-ilang answered back, cutting in with a justification to her statement.

"Your *Tata* seems to be indifferent but he's a good father to you. He loves you, my dear child."

Normally Ilang-ilang wouldn't have talked back at her *Nana*, but she believed it was time to let her know how she felt, so she blurted out without reservations, "his love chokes, *Nana*. If he loves me he would not have been too insensitive.... and he should have respected all those men who showed interests in me. Look at how they stayed far away, intimidated."

Her nana's voice raised in defense to her father , "Ha! Your *Tata* acted that way because you're still young to have any serious relationship with men. Besides he hasn't seen any here in Opon who is worthy of becoming a good husband to you."

"I'm nineteen, *Nana*," she countered in her coldest tone.

"But you're still a baby!"

"Baby? How old were you when you run away with *Tata*? Nineteen!! You almost forgot that you were as young as I am."

Flabbergasted by the unanticipated outburst of petty exchanges he*r nana* threw a startled glance but wisely said nothing.

Without saying anything more, Ilang-ilang ran to her room and sobbed in bed with exasperation. Later, her senses woke her up from that little confrontation with *nana* when she heard her sneaked behind to follow. She heard the sound of her footsteps and pretended not to know. Nana drew the curtain of her room a little, momentarily to peek inside. Ilang-ilang could feel her sadness. Her mother felt remorse their conversation had ended that way. Ilang-ilang was sobbing and appeasing her was out of timing, so nana left her alone and closed the door behind her. Coupled with exhaustion from the trip, and without changing clothes Ilang-ilang slid into deep sleep.

CHAPTER 37

Realizing that majority of the men were already in their cots, Jonas checked if the captain was in his cabin. He was at the poop busy in a meeting with his crew. This gave him a light of hope and was thrilled at the opportunity. He was gripped with a strong urge, with no more control of himself than to stop the waves from coming. He had not see the moon or the stars above nor heard the rushing of the waves; Jonas was lost in the inner sanctum of his thoughts. He slid into his uncle's cabin, now sure that nobody was watching and taking advantage of the night, closed the door slowly behind and walked on tiptoe. He stopped and listened for any sound. He spotted the box immediately there at the corner where it stood solitarily. In darkness it glowed even more. So he went closer to see if he could open it with a knife. His heart was thumping against his ribs. When he got as close as he could, he swore he heard a clattering, rumbling and scrapping sound inside the box. His heart shot up, he backed away and slipped out as fast as he could away from the cabin.

In that evening his sleep was light, it bothered him terribly. It was upsetting, his stomach churned. Could there be a living creature inside? He got up the following day groggy and weary. When they saw each other at the capstan, he couldn't wait to come out with it to Daniel.

"I slept little last night," he said, with eyes bloodshot.

"Well, me neither. That person next to me was coughing all night," replied Daniel.

"I've got to tell you something, Daniel," he said in whispers to his friend.

"I hope it's not bad."

"No it isn't, but something strange had happened to me. Did you notice a box at the captain's cabin?"

"I didn't. Why? What about it?"

He looked around and with a voice so subdued explained what he had seen and heard to Daniel. "You have to see it before you believe it, but it's a mysterious box. I had been on its heels since we were still in Seville. It had glowed at the seams in the dark and when I was about to open it, I heard some noises as if something was alive inside."

"It must be your imagination. Where did you see the glow coming out?"

"It's a closed box with no openings. The glow came out from the seams, at the sides. I was at the point of opening it but when I heard the noises I ran out of the cabin."

His disclosure was profoundly disturbing to his friend, as well.

"Hmm . . . that's curious! Were you careful nobody saw you going inside?"

"I'm sure nobody saw me came out."

"Were you able to open the box and see what's inside?"

"No, as I said, I was about to open it," affirmed Jonas , so certain of his statement, and whispering very low.

"Chess any one," interrupted Luis, who emerged suddenly from the kitchen. His naughty grin gave Jonas a little jolt.
With unusual equanimity he was quick to recover from the surprise.

"Oh, it's you Luis! Are you free now? Daniel here could play with you. I still have to do some chores at the kitchen. Maybe this afternoon after work I could burn two games with you."

"Well . . . I've done my part. Hey, could I to talk to you if I'm not intruding Jonas?" Luis' tone was serious.

"Of course," Daniel wink when he excused himself. Jonas fitted one pellet stretched the rubber and release it. The can on top of the railing clink and he knew his aim was still as good as before.

"I was reminded years back, when I went to Valencia on a vacation, of a certain fact about the people. No offense. Is it true that people in Valencia eat rats, Luis?"

"That's an exaggerated story about Valencia, Jonas. Some people working in rice fields may be. And they only eat those in rice fields." His eyebrows winced.

"I heard some men here were bent on catching them for barbecue," Jonas kidded.

"I never thought about that in that light. But I can't stop them if they're hungry," Luis annoyed at the baseness of his innuendo dropped his answer without reservation.

"Tell me Jonas, somebody saw you got into the captain's cabin. Is it true?" His tone changed, and logic told him that Jonas was a little bit irked at the accusation.

"It's none of their business, Luis."

"It's my business and I'm concerned. What did you do alone inside?" Luis' tone was reproachful.

"If I told you would it change the situation?"

"Of course, at least I could defend you. There are some men out there who think that you are stealing something inside. …food perhaps?"

"They are paranoid. If there's food inside then it would only be enough for one meal, besides food is within our reach at the kitchen anytime we go hungry. That's the privilege we have working to prepare everybody's meal. You know that pretty well, Luis. How can they think of such an absurd idea?"

"You should be careful nobody catches you next time, or they'll resort to violence."

When he was about to leave, Jonas decided to tell him some truth of what he did. He opened up, "it's not food. It's something else. It was my curiosity. I wanted to know something that's inside."

It stopped him short, "Then tell me what it is, if it's not food. The truth will set you free."

"It's about an oak box I had been dying to uncover its secret. It glowed at the seams as if there was a strong light inside."

"Huh, how strange! You could have asked the captain to make it easier." His eyes grew wide, still doubting Jonas' statement.

"I would. It's only that my desire to discover it first overruled my judgment."

"Alright then, I believe you. I'll check it out myself. Be extremely careful."

They parted ways, leaving Jonas to contemplate on the seriousness of what was about to befall upon him from the hands of some men, unmindful of the dangers of pursuing such foolish curiosity. This gave him a shiver down his spine. He was grateful Luis warned him timely.

Luis and Daniel advised him against pursuing the little foolishness he had been doing for some time. He admitted they were right and that his curiosity could lead him to trouble, but he justified to himself that this was how his mind worked. It lessened the boredom that was seeping into him. It was a comfort knowing a trade-off by being curious and concerned would come afterwards.

CHAPTER 38

In the afternoons Jonas always tried to catch a nap. If sleep was difficult, he always imagined being in a tropical island with plenty of food, lying in a hammock under a coconut tree and enjoying life's remaining fantasies.

Whenever he opened his eyes, his imaginings vanished and saw himself drifting back to reality, wallowing in the middle of a vast timeless expanse. At night when he dreamed, it's dreadfully terrifying. Shadows from the moon, from a lamp, the mast, someone's figure or the shadows of hairy rats followed him wherever he went. Then there's one in his dreams which was ever more frightening, it lingered. He was running away but gaining no distance, his pace exceptionally slow. He fell and struggled to pull himself up, but it caught his right foot. Wriggling and kicking from its grasps he couldn't free himself. Shadows deepened. The nibbling at his feet grew faster. Wanting to know what it was he forced his eyes to open but they wouldn't let him . An overpowering fear was building inside him, a voice saying wake up, wake up Jonas. He sat up and snapped himself into awareness. When his eyes finally opened , there, before him at the foot of his bed, he saw a black rat as big as a cat with big round eyes staring at him, its shadow on the wall. He kicked as hard as he could several times until it jumped out from the bed and darted away, as shocked as he was. Jonas woke up from that horrible nightmare, sweating. It started with the oak box. He had finally opened it and some reddish serpent jumped out towards him. He told himself to run, but his leg was caught by its large teeth. Now breathing deeply, he was thankful it was only a dream.

This made him step out into the upper deck to take some fresh air and release his fears. Far away he could see some dolphins cruising along the side of the galleons. He looked up and saw the captain talking with the Commander at the poop. His business must be of vital importance otherwise the Commander would not have come personally. Seldom had he been on board unless for a really good reason. Then Jonas learned that everybody was summoned to an assembly at the quarterdeck.

Not so long after, the junior and senior officers, members of the crew, the captain and the Commander who came from *Trinidad*, the mother ship, milled into the quarterdeck. Daniel and Jonas found themselves seated at the capstan waiting for the Captain's announcement. The rest of the men were crammed together to listen to what he would say.

"Men, I hope you have rested well."
Everybody roared in disagreement.

"You might be wondering why we are gathered here today. Some of you might already know. This is the reason the commander is here to talk it out with me. We are encountering a major problem. Many of us are getting sick and some are seriously ill. I've had some consultations with the doctor and he told me that there's a way to prevent this from getting out of hand. I have requested Doctor Santos, here, seeing that with his authority he is the most capable person to talk to you about it," captain Serrano after opening, transferred the floor to the doctor.

"Good morning to everyone. I don't know if I would say good morning because it isn't. We have a big problem and if we don't arrest this problem we would keep on losing men. Let's go to the bottom of this problem, the origin. There are so many of them now, attracted by the stock of food that we have at the hold. I would suggest that we eradicate them once and for all," the doctor announced.

Most of the men nodded in agreement to what he said.

"That's the reason the Commander is here with us now. He wants us to implement an immediate solution to this problem. There are sixty one of us in this galleon. We would divide ourselves into groups and start the attack as soon as we adjourn this meeting. Arm yourselves with sticks and clubs. I want none of them to be left and propagate again. Open up all covered places and nooks where you think they could hide, at the hold and at the bilge. Open all walls and spaces in between." ordered the captain.

"Do you have any questions or suggestions?"

"*Señor*, sticks and clubs are fine if they are out facing us. But they are hidden somewhere. We should think of a way to get them out," said Daniel, who stood to speak up.

"Men, what do you think? That statement of Daniel is practically correct."

"Fire, *Señor*, we should use fire. We'll scare them with fire so that they'd come out of hiding," volunteered one soldier.

"What if somebody's not careful and he sets fire to the ship instead," objected the second mate.

"*Señor*, we could use sound. Banging and clanging may bring them out," stated Daniel.

"I agree to all of your suggestions but let's be extremely vigilant. Fire and sound are just fine. Anymore questions?"

"Sir, I have. I have a phobia of rats. Will I be exempted from this exercise?" one soldier implored.

Some jeering and scoffing from the crowd followed after his remark.

"They won't bite you. No, there won't be any exceptions. If you wouldn't do it, the more you'd be suffering," the captain responded.

"Do you have any more questions?"

"*Señor*, the root of our problem is not the existence of the rats," a resounding comment came from the capstan.

All people shifted their eyes on the speaker who was Jonas.

"It is only an offshoot to the main problem, a branch that protrudes from the main trunk. The real problem is something else. If we cut a branch it would still grow back," he asserted with so much fervor, that everybody was enthralled listening, wanting to grasp the meaning of what he had just said.

"Then, can you tell us what the real problem is, Jonas, so that we could move on from here," captain Serrano emphatically interrupted Jonas' intelligent assessment of the problem.

"After eradicating them, we follow it up with the cleaning of the bilge and the lower deck. It does not stop there. It is important that each one of us should clean our cots every day and maintain personal hygiene. The root of all this is our attitude towards hygiene, *señor*," he stressed his point so clearly that the commander was impressed instantly.

"Good observation," the commander cut-in, smiling widely at Jonas and nodded. It was clear he was satisfied with his comment.

The captain waited for anyone to raise a question. He scanned at everyone's weary faces, shifted to the commander, then to Jonas and continued.

"Men our enemies are intelligent. Be sure to open all places where they could hide, at the bilge, at the kitchen and the hold where we keep the provisions. Rats will eat almost anything, so keep your spaces clean and don't leave food out. Make it a point that your cots and the storage areas are clean and dry. Close up small holes and cracks they can hide themselves through. Also remember Jonas' suggestion. I will repeat. Maintain cleanliness and personal hygiene all the time. If there are no questions, then let's start moving after them."

CHAPTER 39

They peeped through the window, Asma and Ilang-ilang, to see who were singing. The moon lingered in the sky yet its beam was so pale they couldn't make out who were singing. Almost every night admirers come and go to serenade, different ones each time, identifiable only through their voices. Most of the time they were not the admirers but singers accompanying them, so it was difficult to guess who was who, and who was proposing. Sometimes their singings were irritatingly out of tune.

"*Sa imong gugma* . . ." The song ended and the three young men went away with their song.

"Who was that, my dear child?" inquired Yaya Nabilah who was kneading rice dough for *bibingka* cake.

"They were those in the neighbourhood, Yaya, I couldn't make out who they were."

"One of your admirers, Ilang-ilang," cut-in Asma, Yaya's eighteen year old daughter who was helping her mother with the dough, rolling the mixture with her hands.

"They're here almost every night. But I think some come for you, Asma," Ilang-ilang said teasingly.

Asma giggled and wiped the little rice flour that smudged her arm with her apron.

"Serenading is common among admirers who don't have the faces to show. That is why they profess their love at night partly hidden in the darkness," said Yaya Nabilah in the process of cutting pieces of banana leaves .

"…not very good admirers. Next time I would go down and invite them to come in, don't you think so Ilang-ilang," she continued.

"I don't think they would come to show their faces," Asma who was now sprinkling her creation with cheese, shook her head.

"You've been a lot of help, Asma," Ilang-ilang said. Asma smiled at the compliment.

"Who were those kids, Nabilah," inquired *Tata* who joined them unexpectedly, coming out from his room.

"They were Ilang-ilang's admirers, Datu," said Nabilah . She finished cutting the leaves then laid the scissors down on the table.

"Next time they come, and they don't show their faces do something."

"Invite them in? They wouldn't."

"Then throw urine at them so that they would come back no more." Then he slid back to his room hunching.

Yaya Nabilah stopped what she was doing and looked at Ilang-ilang who was not at all surprised at the comment. She defended her father when he was gone, "I think your father was only joking Ilang-ilang."

"That wasn't nice of him to say that," said Asma in a whisper.

"Long time ago he actually did that, when some admirers serenaded his sister. He ended up with a fight," disclosed yaya Nabilah.

Ilang-ilang shrugged her shoulders and proceeded to her room for the night.

"Thank you for reminding me that but I know the story yaya. Good night," nonchalant, she then slipped inside .

Asma put the rolled dough on a pan, made some final touches pressing uneven surfaces with her fingers then introduced it inside the flaming clay oven.

CHAPTER 40

Tension had set in among the men and several skirmishes erupted due to the lack of food and water. Grumbling among the ranks indicated an undercurrent of uneasiness which flowed down to the lower echelons. Fighting was common.

In the other ships, there were men who were up against the commander. Hunger and fatigue sapped a large portion of the men's patience. The captains of the galleons refused to take orders from him as a sign of protest.

Then one night some of the men were slowly eliminated one after the other, punished for disobeying orders.

It was spring the 20th of the month, vernal equinox year 1520, when they arrived at the port of Saint Julian. The sky was clear. From then on the Commander ordered that they stay close along the coast. The air was still cold from the north and Jonas saw Daniel on deck at the capstan still wearing his winter jacket. He heard some men coughing at the sides.

Daniel coughed a fake one. "Morale of the men is awfully low," he whispered.

"I can't blame them," Jonas coughed himself, imitating Daniel.

"Yeah, some got into trouble because of lack of food; they sometimes got themselves into a fight." Daniel pulled his jacket together, to cover his neck from the cold winds.

"Did you hear three of the ships rose up against the Commander their captains were bent on taking him back to be arrested, saying he was leading them all to destruction?" Daniel said, rubbing his hands together desperately to keep them warm.

"I heard it," Jonas affirmed, shivering with cold.

"However, through the help of his assistant and some men whom he carried with him, the commander was able to save the three ships."

"Yeah, I'm glad he recovered," this time Jonas coughed, not feigning anymore for the cold was real.

"I heard the captain of one of them, Luis de Mendoza, was punished and executed by a party sent by the Commander."

"I think some will go to court when we get back to Spain." Sensing that the cold was getting worse, Jonas signaled for them to go inside.

"After recovering the three ships the captain of one of the ship, Gaspar Quesada, was also punished by death five days later."

He went first then Daniel followed down the stairs.

While going down towards the lower deck he was honestly concerned to know about the captain and asked, ". . . and how about your uncle Juan?"

"I don't think he would do that. He's too conventional," Jonas retorted, in defense of the captain.

Going into their cots, the conversation continued, "a mutiny...that's critical if we're in the middle of a crisis. We should be united, together all for one, hand in hand, to ride it through the storms. Stuck it out with the Commander because he's the only one who knows where we are going."

"I hope it will never happen to us." They passed the narrow aisle that led to the cots which were arranged permanently pegged side by side and heard some men coughing.

Then Daniel slumped on his cot, "farfetched, but it will if things don't improve. The morale of the men is already at the lowest and provisions are running low. It's wearing patience thin. If there's a mutiny it would be coming from the ranks not from the captain himself."

Jonas nodded to agree with what he said. He was standing beside him and remembered the carrot sticks in his jacket where they were hidden. He flushed them out and gave them to him, "here take these. They're good. We have no sandwich today because the supply of flour is being rationed."

Daniel was looking around and with a low voice sought for an answer, "Where did you get them?"

"They were in a sack in the kitchen coming from the other ships," Jonas told him with all honesty.

Joy revealed itself on his face when he smiled at the gift. "I don't know if you weren't around, my friend, I would have been among those who got sick."

Daniel expressed his concern on the severity of scurvy disease to all the patients he had been visiting. He said they had skin sores and swelling gums; it seemed to him like leprosy. After thanking Jonas with a tight squeeze of the hand, he hid the carrots.

"*De nada*, but be discreet with it," cautioned Jonas anew.

". . . by the way, happy birthday Daniel."

CHAPTER 41

Cool winds puffed at the flapping canvas sails on the mast above, edging the *Santiago* reasonably forward and the soothing sounds of surfs barging at the side of the galleon indicated it was a fine day for sailing.

"Hey, nobody's inside the cabin. My uncle is up there. Let's go and see open the box once and for all, Daniel. I couldn't sleep thinking."

"You should stop this madness, Jonas," Daniel looked at his friend reprovingly.

"I can't. It's nagging me and I have to finish it now. I promise you nothing will happen. We've been through more difficult times before. This is spinach."

"Ok . . . now, tell me what we should do as soon as we know its contents. Take it out?"

"We'll decide afterwards."

"I've been behaving correctly so far, Jonas. If we fucked up, your uncle wouldn´t think twice in throwing us in the ocean. Now I'm sure of that."

"Just follow me."

"I won't do it!" he stood firmly.

"Come on, Daniel. Nothing will happen to us. I assure you."

Still Daniel resisted but his voice became weaker and weaker, "Oh, Jonas you're pulling me like a puppet. I cannot do it."

"We've been through in all of this since the beginning. What is one last time? Do it for me Daniel."

Then he buckled, "Oh, what the heck. Let's see if it's clear, okay? I'll follow. But, hey, let's be careful."

The captain's cabin was so close to the capstan and slipping in darkness would only be for a second. They checked around to see if somebody was watching. When they saw it was clear Jonas jumped down and went inside first, then Daniel tiptoed behind. Breathing heavily, he looked around, heart thumping loudly.

The box was nowhere to be found, not in its usual place, nor at the corner where it used to be. Jonas pointed at the exact site where it was standing. It was there at the corner below the world map. They searched thoroughly but the box was gone. Desperation set in.

"Cross my heart it was right there, at the corner. This tall . . . and this thick," Jonas showed Daniel its size by using his hands to show him the height and thickness.

Daniel was relieved nothing came out of their little mischief. "Are you sure? Let's go out before somebody comes and catches us here."

Without further waste of time, they slipped out as fast as they could and closed the cabin door behind. The only reason for its disappearance was its transfer to the other ships or it may have been taken by someone.

"I think I saw it transferred to the *Trinidad* by some of your uncle's trusted men."

"Are you positive it was the same box?"

"The same size you showed me. Your uncle didn't leave it out of sight until it was hauled into the skiff. That's why I presumed it was the same box. Didn't you see it?"

"Unbelievable! Of all the so many boxes coming in and out to the other galleons, why that box in particular?"

"You must have been at the kitchen when it was carried away. Besides you had mentioned it was addressed to the Commander. Your uncle was only the care taker."

"Now it would be difficult for us to know what's inside," Jonas sighed deeply, as if he had lost something of value. Indeed he lost something: he lost the opportunity to satisfy his curiosity.

CHAPTER 42

It was a hot day and the sun was high with little thin clouds moving slowly beyond the horizon. One was at the crow's nest looking out for land, another mopping the deck floor, two were talking, and some were looking far away into the vast ocean. Jonas was at the upper deck playing chess with Luis when he was told to go see the captain. In a few seconds, he knocked, hesitant to open the door, and then pushed it without even waiting for an answer. The musky odor of his uncle's tobacco filled the room.

"You sent for me, *tío*?"

"Sit down Jonas," ordered Captain Juan Serrano in his usual air of fairness.

Jonas was uneasy and anxious. "What could this be this time?" the question flashed across his mind. "Could it be that he found out about the sandwiches? Or somebody must have told him about me going into his cabin?" he speculated.

"When I saw you here on your first day, I thought heaven would come down on me. Stowing away is punishable," he started his admonition, so it seemed to Jonas that his feeling was right. "It's now time he would bring down the ax," swore Jonas to himself.

"Please, *tío*," he was almost pleading.

"Haven't you noticed that I haven't handed down the punishment? I was observing you, Jonas," the captain grunted.

"Now it's my end," he resigned to his fate.

"Now relax. I'm giving you a chance. I've seen that you were behaving well. And at the meeting the commander commended your exemplary behavior. He had decided favorably and said you could stay."

Jonas was open-mouthed. He was bent on doubting the intentions of such promotions. Was there such thing as purging of the soul? They had committed an offense by stowing away and he believed that because of this Daniel and he should be punished, not to be given a reprieve or pardon. He thought his uncle must be bluffing.

"What is the implication of what he said," he inquired tethering on the edge of breaking down with relief. His uncle didn't have the slightest idea that he was shivering inside.

"You could stay with a higher status. The commander is looking for people who could be loyal to him. That's the reason he was giving this privilege to you."

"And?" he still doubted.

"That means you're now entitled to all the privileges the rest of the men are enjoying."

"Can you please elaborate, *señor*?"

"There's a mutiny going on. He has chosen you as one of his eyes and ears."

"And . . . what do I get in doing that?"

"You'll become a regular. You can have uniforms and be entitled to a stipend." When he said this Jonas almost fell out of his chair.

"Does that mean I would be out of the kitchen?"

"No. I think you'll be safe there. You'll still be working with Jose and I order you to continue doing your job well."

"Thank you, *señor*."

"Now, when you see Daniel, tell him to come here."

"*Si, señor*."

"I'm not finished yet, Jonas," he stopped and turned back.

"The commander is wary of loyalty. He thinks that some men are planning something more disastrous, all over the five ships. I'm afraid that this rebellious spirit would destroy the principal purpose of what we came here for. Did you hear some were already punished?"

"What could I do in order to help?"

"I want you to observe. If you see or heard something unusual, report to me immediately. Is that clear?"

"*Si, señor*."

"Now, tell Daniel to come."

When he came out Jonas was brimming with joy. Finally his patience had borne him some fruits. He mused with excitement. He told Daniel to go and see the captain without telling him of the details of his conversation. He went practically running.

"Sit down Daniel. Do you know why I called for you?"

"No, señor."

"I would have punished you for stowing, but we need people with your caliber who know something about medicine. Doctor Santos is contented with your performance. He said that you ought to be given the same privilege as the other men here. I have also been observing you, and I saw that you were doing all your responsibilities religiously. I had recommended your promotion to the commander and he approved it . . . congratulations."

"*Gracias señor.*"

"Where exactly in Madrid are you from, Daniel?"

"We lived in an apartment near *Puerta Del Sol*, but my family came from Alcala de Henares, *señor*."

"Nice place. I heard there are some promising writers in that place."

"Yeah, I think one famous writer will come out from that place, *señor*. One of my relatives has already been showing some genius in his writings, but the opportunity to have his work published is so rare nowadays."

"I see . . . they must have already missed you."

"We are so many in the family, *señor*, six siblings. Yes, I had some fun with my brothers and sisters, but I had to decide. I am the third and moving out was the only thing I could do to help my parents."

"Alright . . . now, you don't have to worry about your punishment."

"I don't understand, *senor*," Daniel was faking. The tip Jonas had given him after his talk with the captain was enough for him to gain confidence.

"Because of this promotion you are now entitled to a monthly compensation. Call it whatever you want but it's a stipend. You can save your ducats and when you go back to Madrid you'll have something to start with. Now go to the requisition officer for your uniforms," continued Captain Serrano.

"*Gracias, señor.*"

"Do you have any questions?"

Daniel only moved his head left and right to mean no, then stood up to leave.

"I hope you would keep on doing what you have been doing, in the same manner and in the same spirit, Daniel."

"I will live up to your expectations, *señor.*"

"One more thing, Daniel. Have you heard of any rebellious spirits in the ranks?"

"There are some grumblings among the men."

"I want you to be on the look-out. There are some men who are planning another mutiny. The Commander is picking out loyal men to be his eyes and ears and I have chosen you and Jonas. So if you heard of any dissent among the people, report immediately. Is that clear?"

"*Si, señor.*"

"When you see Luis Mendoza, tell him to come."

"*Si, señor.*"

The motive of the promotions wasn't difficult to understand. The commander was desperate to find people who were more committed to the cause, eyeing men who had the tendency to lean on their side with unwavering loyalty. He knew that being the nephew of his most trusted man Jonas would more likely be loyal to the mission. And Daniel, being Jonas' friend would easily be influenced by their friendship. Clearly, the motive was to preserve the sole purpose of the mission, and that was to eventually find the source of the spicy cloves.

CHAPTER 43

One Saturday night, some men positioned themselves below their window evidently to serenade. One started strumming the ektara, a one stringed instrument and the singing drifted into the cool night then faded nicely. After the first song, came discordant voices which were clearly from those under the influence of alcohol, and the singing erupted into a hubbub, coarse and irritating. *Tata* was in his room resting when the singing went pitiably this way. He went out of his room tromping madly towards the *ibuh rumah* where everybody was gathered. That was the first time Ilang-ilang saw her father so raving mad at a very insignificant matter.

"I won't put up with this noise anymore. Next time they come to serenade, they'll learn who the Datu is."

"Nabilah, you know what to do."

"Datu, please, I can't do it."

"If you can't, then I would do it," snorting, he trudged towards the kitchen, with a burning desire to do something.

"They must be some guys from another village. Otherwise they would have made themselves known," commented yaya Nabilah.

"Yeah, young men in Opon are respectful," said Asma.

Then *tata* came hunching back with a bucket of water mixed with some vinegar in it and without second thoughts tossed the mixture out of the window to the men below.

One shouted some expletives. Seconds later a stone thudded onto the wall of the *ibuh rumah* and rolled on the floor. Unmistakably, one of the men pelted a stone in return for the water.

"Who do they think they are, throwing a stone at us? This is a clear outrageous affront to my authority," *Tata* hollered.

"If you hadn't splashed urine at them they wouldn't have responded so indifferently," said *nana*, who was now with them at the *ibuh rumah*.

". . . urine with stones? I thought it would be urine with urine and stones with stones? And it was only water!"

"Oh, *Tata* they are merely young boys," pleaded *nana*.

"Yes, but young boys should also learn some respects."

"*Akmal* let's go down and see who they are and teach these bastards some basic lessons."

All they heard afterwards were loud voices, running and some commotions. Something was going on downstairs. The following morning, they learned one of those who serenaded was badly wounded in the skirmish. That's how fierce the Datu was, most of the time going into a fight with the least provocation. Tonight he had been converted into a monster.

Sometimes Ilang-ilang wondered if that was the reason he became a Datu in Opon, by ruling the people with an iron hand, showing them who was the authority. All brawn he wasn't, though. He had also a soft spot in him, which was a complete opposite of what he had shown, generous and kind. And because of this generosity and kindness people regarded him in diverse levels, yet most respected him for being tough and severe.

CHAPTER 44

The galleons were still moored at the port of Saint Julian when the clouds got thicker and darker. Beads of rain trickled down the window pane at the poop. Jonas was mopping the floor and noticed a bottle rolling over and over. He looked up and knew something was coming. The unusual swaying of *Santiago* was unmistakable. Tides slammed on their sides in loud splashing booms that brought foams of salt water into the deck. Then he heard the bleating of the crew.

"Lower the sails . . . lower the sails! Storm is coming," the first mate shouted, seeing a gust of wind was about to bombard *Santiago* like canons.

The wind got stronger and stronger and *Santiago* swayed terribly on its sides. When Jonas looked out the other galleons were likewise in the same situation bobbing in and out of the big waves. He was resigned to the idea that the other galleons could do something to help them for the looks of it they had to save themselves first before the others.

"We can't hold on, *señor*. We're not going to make it," shouted the first mate, who felt the swaying was getting stronger.

Jonas saw everything. The ship rammed into a big rock and shuddered. There was a loud crack followed by the rushing of water that gushed its way into the lower deck and the bilge. He rushed down to check the damage and saw the gaping hole as big as a barrel. Water was unstoppable, rushing, filling all the spaces below. *Santiago* was sinking.

"Jump overboard and head for the shore," cried the captain.

"We've hit a big rock. Men brace yourselves."

"We're going down," somebody at the deck yelled.

"Abandon ship, abandon ship," the captain ordered everybody to leave the ship right away.

After battling the winds and seeing that the ship was sinking everybody swam to shore. When they reached the shore, all of them laid down on the sand exhausted. Turning back, they all witnessed *Santiago* sinking down slowly to the bottom, stern first, followed by the body then the bow. As it slipped down gradually, bubbles of water formed around the remaining last part of the bow to create a whirlpool, then volumes of water rushed inside to follow the bow.

That was the last time they saw of *Santiago*.

Not long after, boxes and crates of provisions started popping out one by one above the water floating, together with their personal belongings. After the shock and exhaustion they were gathered together and an assessment followed.

"Make a head count," shouted the captain.

The counting was followed snappily and the report of the first mate came afterwards.

"Everybody counted. No casualties, *señor*."

"Good. I want this to be done rapidly. Now let's save all we could and transfer them to the other ships," ordered the captain who was standing on the beach, his gaze at the boxes floating on the water.

Daniel had seen all of it, too. He witnessed that the portside of *Santiago* careened sideways and rammed into the rocky shore. He heard a loud crushing sound then saw that water seeped into the decks, volumes of water rushed in until almost all of the lower deck was inundated. It sank lower and he decided he would have to jump into the water and head for the shore. The wind battered *Santiago* terribly it swayed and tilted on its side. At the shore he saw the stern tipped and the ship dipped slowly to the bottom.

When the wind had dissipated the captain and all of the crew started moving. Men were transferred to *Trinidad* and *Victoria*, including Daniel and Jonas along with the merchandise, artillery and fittings that were still usable. In this same port they repaired the other ships. The other bigger galleons survived but needed some repairs.

"After the transfers all of us were crammed into small places I couldn't take a rest, I'd rather be on deck," complained Daniel.

"Hold on my friend. We have to hang on to whatever we have in order to survive. Good thing I was still assigned at the kitchen. Here I brought you something," Jonas encouraged him, seeing that his spirit was low.

"*Gracias amigo.* I'm sorry my patience went to the limits."

"Did you hear about the promotion of Alvaro Mesquita?"

"What about the Portuguese?"

"He's now captain of one of the remaining ships. I think the Commander is now putting people whom he trusts more."

"Do you trust that decision yourself?"

"I'm reserving my comments until we see how he performs. So far he's been so kind to his men."

". . . and your uncle?"

"He's in *Trinidad* with the commander, as his side kick."

"I'm glad your uncle is with the Commander."

"Yeah, I share the same opinion."

"What could have happened to the oak box, I wonder. It must be safe in *Trinidad* with the Commander."

". . . and the damned rats? They should have gone down to the bottom, too. Their squeaking, grinding and scraping, which penetrated the walls nightly, all of them gone to rest at the bottom of the sea."

CHAPTER 45

  Black wood or charcoal was common in Sugbo, used by people for cooking, ironing or barbecuing. In their native tongue they called them *uling*. Around the market most of what you see was black wood or charcoal or *uling* on display. It's cheap and food tasted better cooked with it. Even rice was better cooked in black wood than in any other way.

  Ilang-ilang was with *Nana* and the household helpers to do their weekly marketing, going around getting the best price. *Nana* was the best haggler and she could get almost half of the price down all the time. They always brought with them baskets and baskets of eggs for haggling.

  They raised plenty of chicken in Opon and supply of eggs was abundant. They barter goods with eggs. That's how they get fruits, vegetables and other supplies- by using eggs. With one basket of eggs *nana* could already supply their pantry for the week with meat, fruits and vegetables. Ilang-ilang learned everything by going with *nana* to market. Some other times *Nana* would tell her to go to the market to get the supplies herself. Over time, with the assistance of Yaya Nabilah and Asma, she did all the bargaining by herself.

"You gave her more eggs than is required," commented *Yaya*, when Ilang-ilang traded for a pair of sandals.

"I cannot be like *Nana*, *Yaya*. I'm too soft to trade."

"You'll learn soon, Ilang-ilang. Remember this: if you think you'll be giving them the entire basket, give them half of it."

"Give them half of what I think is the value?"

"Yes, dear child. Then go up little by little, until you meet half-way. That's how haggling is supposed to be done."

"Well, I didn't mind giving her all in the basket."

"That's because you have plenty. What if you have barely enough and there's no more coming? That's the time you will have to think of your eggs worth, my dear child. The owner of the sandals would think so similarly. She would have willingly parted with them with half of your basket."

"We still have one basket to trade, *Yaya*," uttered Ilang-ilang, moving into a stall displaying different kinds of women's clothing.

"I'd like to have that dress," ordered Ilang-ilang to the stall owner, pointing at a red one on display.

"It's so dainty," said Asma.

"Try it. It's for you Asma, on your birthday. I'm giving it to you as a gift," Ilang-ilang smiled at Yaya Nabilah. It was a subtle gesture in return for the lessons she received on bartering and haggling from Asma's mother.

Asma could hardly believe what she heard from Ilang-ilang and all she could say was, "Thanks a lot." She beamed with joy. That day Ilang-ilang also felt extraordinarily happy for Asma. She learned that giving was more satisfying to the giver than to the receiver, a simple lesson in generosity which had been imprinted indelibly in her heart.

CHAPTER 46

Summer was about to end when the galleons sailed southward from the port of St. Julian. They entered a wide river which they called Santa Cruz. Men were sent to the banks to see if there was something to eat. They found out that there were wild berries and cherries on trees. They picked plenty of them and took as much as they could haul in.

The cargoes of the lost ship were already distributed among the other ships and they continued hauling in provisions which had remained there up to the month of September. They took in water and plenty of fish which they caught in this river. It's autumn and the air was nippy, and the two friends saw each other again.

"Are you fine now, Daniel?"

"Oh, yes . . . I guess it was because of the transfers that I freaked out. It was in fact stressful we had to work days on ends."

"We have plenty of food now, but I can't tell how long it will last, seeing that we still have to sail for months and months."

It's getting cold I fear a lot of us would be getting the flu."

"I heard they're getting in some natives from this river, to act as guides. Tall about nine to ten spans in height and structurally well made. The men who found them said they were savages because they eat raw meat and roam around and have no fixed abode."

"Yeah, I've seen them. How do they survive in this cold?" Daniel asked, to have a reasonable explanation.

"All of them are archers and hunt many animals with arrows. With the animal skins they gather, they dry them under the sun and tailor them after the shape of their body. They wear shoes too, which cover their feet up to the ankles."

"I wonder how they stitch their shoes and their clothing together."

"Well, they say they use flints and sharp stones for their knives to cut. Even the tips of their arrows are made of these, they don't use any irons at all, but I figure that they use bones as needles to sew their clothing."

"And families?"

"They do have families. The women are small and they tuck them with them wherever they go, carrying their heavy burdens on their back together with their flocks and whenever the night found them they set up tents and sleep there."

"Their situation must be more difficult than what little we have here in the galleons."

"I don't think so, because they're used to such kind of living. Did you get your clothes," Jonas inquired seeing how it was getting colder, changing the subject of the conversation.

"I was already freezing, I wondered if I didn't. The chief doctor requested the supply officer to issue us with winter clothing. I got one good jacket and some pullovers."

"I got them, too."

"Last night two men succumbed to scurvy, they were too weak with anemia and had bleeding on their gums and skin. Now we're down to less our number."

"What a waste of human lives," Jonas commented.

"Yeah . . . our body needs fruits and vegetable to be strong, especially to synthesize the collagen found in the skin, without which would trigger bleedings."

"What special things do they have to make us strong?"

"Vitamin C."

"Hmm . . . What do we have to eat in order to get vitamin C, aside from papaya and kiwi which my mother had told me?" Jonas asked.

"Citrus fruits like oranges and lemon and green leafy vegetables, and we don't have that much in our diet for a long time," replied his friend.

"What else?"

"Broccoli is good too. Vitamin C is an essential vitamin for our body. It must be consumed regularly because it isn't stored in the body."

"Hmm . . . I didn't know."

"It is needed for normal growth and development of the skin, tendons and ligaments."

"I see," he answered briefly, but he understood the implications of it all.

"It is also an important antioxidant protecting our cells from damage. As an antioxidant, vitamin C may help protect us from any heart disease," explained Daniel.

CHAPTER 47

The air was getting cooler when the Commander ordered the galleons to take off from Santa Cruz river, sometime in the middle of October. They continued navigating along the coast for three days when they discovered a cape, for which the name Cape of the Eleven Thousand Virgins was given. Then they found themselves at the mouth of a strait they aptly called after the commander. He assigned *Victoria* and *San Antonio* to explore the strait, leaving the *Trinidad* at the mouth.

"Let's enter this strait and see what we can discover. I want six men to go down on two skiffs and see for yourselves," ordered the Commander.

They found three channels, that is to say, two in a southerly direction, and one traversing the country in the direction of *Maluku*. The galleons went further to inquire, and they set sail and anchored at the mouth of the channels.

"Sir, galleon *Victoria* returned to Captain *Alvaro Mesquita*. The other ship, *San Antonio*, entered into one of the bays going to the south, and hasn't returned as yet," reported his second mate."

"Then let's set sail and go southward. Leave a note in those places so that if the other ship returned, it could take the course we would be taking," said the commander.

"The other ship, *San Antonio*, however, deserted and must have returned to Spain, Sir," stated the second officer.

The desertion of *San Antonio* was another blow which hit the commander, but similar to a beaten fighter he carried on, unrelenting to the end. After this the remaining galleons entered into the largest channel during the day, which at some places had a width of about three leagues, and in some places half a league, then they anchored at night.

"It's a huge channel. Send some men to see if there's an opening towards the other side."

After surveying what's ahead the men returned to the flagship bringing some good news.

"*Señor*, there's an outlet towards a broad ocean."

The galleons floated placidly in the stillness of the night. The clouds parted and the light of the moon streamed across the earth to guide them. It was in the months of October to November 1520, when they were cruising in that strait, for exactly thirty six days. And as soon as they went out from the strait, they made their course for the most part, to the northwest, exiting to a vast mass of ocean. Because it was peacefully and placidly overpowering he called it "The Pacific".

Thereafter they celebrated the discovery. Daniel and Jonas saw each other again on the upper deck. The air was cool and Daniel was chilling.

"How are you my friend?" Jonas studied his friend while looking at him bundled up in thick clothing.

His breath steaming out like fog, he mumbled, "I'm fine but a bit lonely. I miss my mum and dad and my girl."

"I missed my family, too, especially my mother."

"Did you leave a girlfriend back home?" Daniel asked Jonas.

"No. Not actually. I had a girl but she was only a friend from school that I went out with, but there was nothing in between. We weren't serious at all. I guess it was because I was still so young and innocent in love and sex," Jonas related the only relationship he had , looking far away to reminisce that time.

"For a relationship to work out you have to put a lot of energy on it, and a lot of time," he added.

"Right . . . but you have to love a girl, to actually love her, if you go through it all."

"Yeah, having a family is a serious thing."

"I think when love hits you the world goes round and round and you'd go dizzy wondering what hits you, you'll sacrifice everything, even to the point of going beyond reasons."

"I did have a girl I left in Madrid. She was about my age, cute and we saw each other every day way back in my college days in Medicine. Maria was the most decent girl I knew who came from a good family, and I wished to marry her, but she wanted to be a doctor first. When we go back the first thing I would do is to marry her," confided Daniel.

"You're lucky you have somebody to look forward to, my friend. I envy you. I don't know where my life would lead me to. Destiny seems to be so hazy as yet."

Jonas glanced at his friend across the capstan, his eyes illumined by the bright moonlight. They were both like little boys who missed their play things at school, who missed their rooms, the people visiting them at the weekend, the small chats, their pets, and the sound of the rain on their roof top.

But what Daniel missed a lot was good food. Good food on the table prepared by his mom. He missed lentils, *cocido, paella, callus a la Madrileña,* the different kinds of cheese and *jamon Serrano.*

Jonas missed his mom and dad, too, and this made him ponder for a while, "she must be now around the house busy doing her daily chores, cooking or cleaning, or resting after a day's work. She must have missed me, too. My dad must be at work. I knew he would never miss me, his prodigal son who went away against his will to foster his dreams of glory, of money, of a better future and, inevitably, to escape from the grim deplorable life in Seville. But I missed him considerably."

CHAPTER 48

The soft afternoon breeze coming from the sea brought some childhood memories to this place. Ilang-ilang with her *nana* were seated on the shore facing the sea, where their hut used to be standing years before. The air was salty whilst refreshing. She used to play in the sand barefooted and picked crabs, which she vividly remembered. Strange as it seemed she saw things her *nana* couldn't, such as the contour of the sea line, rocks and stone formations, the rushing tides and the white foams that stayed on the shore, for she had enjoyed to watch them all her life as a child.

"I love it here, *nana*. We shouldn't have transferred to Opon," remarked Ilang-ilang innocently.
Her mother fought with her emotions to show in her face.
"It's change, the inevitable change, my dear child. Life is full of them. When they came we had to run away. They burned all the huts in this place including ours. There was fighting and so many people perished. We were lucky to have escaped," she reminisced

Ilang-ilang looked at her *nana* and queried, "who were they?"

Her *nana* was quick to respond from her memory, "they were some tribes from the north who speak a different tongue. They came in boats. We from the south stood our ground and resisted their assault. The Sugboanons are brave and strong, my dear child."

"Why did they come, *nana*?"

"You know Sugbo. It's so captivating they wanted to conquer it."

"What motivated them to set fire to our homes and kill our people?"

"Trade and its prosperity. Well, it is strategically located that hurricanes could hardly penetrate the center. This is due to the islands with high mountains that surrounded it. For years there have never been any strong winds that came our way."

"And so?"

"Because of its ideal geographical location trade flourished. It was the result of the traders' feeling of security to be doing business in a safe place. They come without fear of any losses from hurricanes and business prospered."

"I see. Do you think they would still come back?"

"I hope they wouldn't."

"That is the reason your uncle became the Rajah. He fought them bravely. Well, it's been years and the Rajah now has a number of strong followers who fortified Sugbo the more. It has become an important and strong citadel that nobody would dare conquer it anymore. If they came again they would more likely meet a good fight."

"Your Tata fought side by side with the Rajah."

"Did he? I supposed *Tata* was made the Datu of Opon as his reward. Is it right, *nana*?"

"Yeah, it's a bit of a reward. He could have been the Rajah of Sugbo."

"I love Sugbo. It's near to everything: grandma's house and my cousins Dayang and Dana. And the shops sell so many things first."

". . . as if you don't come here regularly."

"That is the reason I consider myself luckier than the other girls in Opon."

"You are . . . Opon is our home now, my child. Remember that. And Sugbo will already be a second home to us. It's getting late. Now we have to go or we'll be traveling in the dark," said her *nana*, who started picking up her things.

CHAPTER 49

Jonas had come to the realization that life in the galleon was simply a brief sojourn to be patiently endured, for someday they would finally find the end to their sufferings. He believed with a definite and firm conviction that he would leave when the right time comes along, and could feel that this was in a near future time. Deep within he had always hoped for something special to come. It was a hope that foreshadowed all the sufferings and scarcities that they had temporarily undergone. It gave added meaning to the monotonous days and made all the backbreaking drudgeries irrelevant. It was this blind conviction that gave him the strength that sustained his life at all times.

One afternoon, he was at the lower deck lying on his cot when he heard shouting from above. There were loud voices and running, feet stomping. Daniel came, flying. Jonas had never seen him so ebullient in days.

"What's going on?" Jonas investigated.

"We got a message from the commander, supplies are coming in today," he was panting.

Daniel's news got him to spring up from his cot in excitement, "Where are they from?" Jonas listened intently.

"They are from the river people brought by *San Antonio*."

"San Antonio?" All his unanswered questions about its whereabouts dawned on him suddenly, "so *San Antonio* did not leave us, after all. I thought they went back to Spain and deserted."

"That's what I understood from the message," Daniel spoke with firmness.

Later that afternoon, two skiffs came back bearing sacks and sacks of vegetables, grains, meat and fruits. As soon as the sacks were hauled in, Jonas found himself too busy ripping the bags and peeling the carrots and potatoes in high spirit.

"We have more than enough here ,Jose."

"It wouldn't last long, but today I want you all to be happy," said the chief cook.

That night they had their first complete heavy meal after months of scarcity. They scooped plenty of white rice, topped with grilled meat and laced with soft potato. Fruits came to close their appetites. It was so filling Jonas' eyes shone with tears. And so did Daniel's . At the side of his vision, he observed men contentedly licking their plates clean. They ate ravenously. On one side he heard shouting and whooping. Somebody slipped a jug of coconut red wine. A glass was passed around and singing started, and for that fleeting moment Jonas felt a rush of real happiness.

Autumn dragged on to winter. It was snowing in 1520 when they were sailing in the broad Pacific heading towards the east. The intense cold made ears and hands numbed Jonas had to rub them all the time. At the poop, they found that their needles varied almost two fourths to the northwest, and as soon as they had navigated thus far for many days, they found two islands which were uninhabited. They ran on until they reached the line, when the Commander announced that now they were in the neighborhood of Maluku, which they learned later to be incorrect. And as he had information that there were no more provisions, he ordered that they should go in a northerly direction to as far as ten or twelve degrees. After five months of sea the mood rose up a bit when they saw land.

"Look there are two islands ahead, we could perhaps anchor in them," said his second mate.

"We've reached as far as thirteen degrees north, and now let's navigate to the west then a quarter southwest for about a hundred leagues," said the first officer.

It's already 5th of March, 1521, and the intense cold tapered as they were approaching the islands. The commander chose the bigger one to anchor. There they met some inhabitants in g-strings, with bows and arrows. Jonas noticed that precautions were not taken against them, until they learned that the natives took away the skiff of the flagship in the dead of the night. They cut the rope with which it was fastened and took it ashore without them being able to prevent the islanders from stealing it. They gave this island the name *Isla de ladrones* (The Isle of Thieves).

The Commander seeing that the skiff was lost, set sail as it was already night, tacking about until the next day. Recovery of the skiff was ordered immediately.
"Get fifty to sixty men on the boats. Then we go down ashore to recover the skiff," the Commander bawled.

When morning broke loose Jonas went out to the upper deck and observed that they anchored at the place where the skiff had been taken. Then he witnessed from afar soldiers burning the whole village killing seven or eight people including women, and recovered the skiff. After obtaining their objective, the men returned to the ships. It took them a whole day of waiting when forty or fifty natives from the same land came and brought plenty of food to make peace with them. As soon as they received the offerings, the galleons departed.

"Set our direction to a quarter southwest," the commander hollered. Over a few days in that bearing the men again erringly thought that they had already located Maluku.
"Lands! Lands!" the watchman at the crow's nest yelled.
And so they spotted lands in that direction, for which they named the Islands of *St. Lazarus*. The Commander decided not to touch at the first island they sighted, and went to touch at another further on which appeared more inviting.
Meanwhile Jonas was on deck with Daniel marveling at the island ahead, lined with coconut trees which looked like matchsticks standing side by side on the seashore.

"Why the name archipelago of St. Lazarus, do you know?" Daniel inquired.

"I honestly can't tell you. It must have something to do with the Commander's bible readings. St. Luke says he was a leper and he had so many skin sores on his body," Jonas said.

"Do you read the bible?"

"I do. And perhaps the Commander thinks that it should be significant to call these islands St. Lazarus because of the men who died of scurvy, in memory of them."

"Yeah . . . but how important is St. Lazarus to have been given this honor?"

"Well . . . the story goes that he was a beggar and went to the door of a rich man, Dives, to beg for some crumbs of food and was driven away. Dives was mean and cruel. He sinned for denying to alleviate the hunger of the needy. When both of them died, Lazarus went to stay beside Abraham in heaven while Dives suffered in hell. Because of the fires in hell and the heat that tormented him, Dives prayed to Abraham for him to be able to cool his tongue by asking for water."

"Is it a sin by not giving anything to the beggar?"

"Abraham denied his request. You know what Karma in Buddhism is? It's the same as the Golden rule, which says that if you deny something to one person, a denial would also come upon you in some future time in this lifetime or in the next life somewhere else, like heaven. Dives was denied water for failing to do something on earth."

"Carry on, please," Daniel's interest was kindled.

"Then Abraham said, Dives this is not possible anymore because of the iniquities between you and Lazarus. During your lifetime you received all the good things while he suffered in want and you denied him even with what little you could have shared, to him who didn't have anything."

"Please go on."

"Then Dives prayed that because of this, he wanted to send a warning to his five rich brothers who were left on earth so that they would be warned that what happened to him would also befall to them, if they didn't repent and change."

"*Hmm* . . . there are two Lazarus mentioned in the bible. Is this the one who had dogs following him and licking his sores?"

"Yeah . . . he is the one."

"That's and eye opener!"

"That's why he named these the Islands of St Lazarus," concluded Jonas of his story.

When the galleons approached land, the Commander sent a skiff to shore to scout and see if there were people.

"There are natives. I see two of them," the watchman at the crow's nest cried out.

"Call the men back," ordered the Commander upon hearing the watchman.

The people of the island seeing that the skiff was returning to the galleons, also turned back inland. When the skiff reached the ships, they at once set sail for another island which was so close to this island, and gave it the name The Island of Good Signs, because gold was found in it. Later they learned this was the island of *Limasawa* (which means five wives). They anchored. While they were thus anchored at this island, there came two natives, and brought them meat and coconuts, and told them that they had already seen similar men before them. They were friendly and informed the commander of another island where they could secure plenty of food and provisions to supply them for the remaining days of the expedition.

CHAPTER 50

And hence forth they continued cruising further on among the many islands and ran on to another island which was twenty leagues from that from which they sailed, and came to anchor at another island, which they learned later as Sugbo. It was springtime when they spotted Sugbo. Back in Spain, flowers would have started to blossom and trees turned greener. In this part of the world spring was a strange word, and people only had two seasons: either sunny or rainy days. It was hot and humid when they approached the island. At the kitchen Jose wiped the sweat from his brows while the men at the deck fanned themselves to reduce the effect of the searing heat.

Five men went down to the beach on a skiff to see if it was safe. All of them donned their corselets and head gears in spite of the heat, for protection. With the commander's interpreter, they rowed forward, slowly edging to the unknown, each one uncertain of what they would find ahead.

Waves rushed to shore forming white foams and bubbles as they receded to sea, a hundred boats bobbed over the water and coconut leaves swayed on tall trees, with hanging coco fruits rotting to fall on the ground. A log there, coral stones somewhere, scattered sea shells, seahorses, crawling crabs - all this welcomed the men's sight as they landed.

As soon as they were on the beach, their before them were four natives on gee strings, who had been roasting boar on a long bamboo pole, rolling it over and over, on all sides, to produce an even color. The roasted meat shone red and oil dripped down onto the charcoal fire, producing smoke that filled the air. The smell was so good the intruding men felt hungry.

Natives were on the whole exceptionally friendly but strange people, sometimes timid and at other times extremely aggressive. These before them were harmless, so they came to realize, when upon seeing them automatically kneeled down and bowed their heads.

The men were astonished at the extra ordinary respect the natives had shown them.

"These people must have believed we're some aliens from other planets," one soldier commented.

Another offered an explanation, "Perhaps, it's because of our corselets and helmets."

Without a scintilla of doubt the natives were led to believe so by their strange appearance: tall, pale, bearded, blond haired and heavy with their armors. Everything in them were new and godly. The poor gee stringers thought they were Gods in all respects, and couldn't be fitting and indifferent from the *Ginoos* they believed in.

"*Buenos días,*" one of the soldiers said good morning.

"*Hola,*" another said hello.

No answer. In that fleeting of a second, the natives were caught in a string of perplexing realization in sound and sight. What they heard were also astoundingly out of the ordinary, sounds they never ever had heard before, they could swear they were from outer space.

The five men received only mute responses. They closed distance carefully moving so as not to arouse any feelings of fight or flight. So again it was hand movements. They were like deaf mutes, desperate to communicate. Good thing the guide of Maluku was there to make it easier for them. However he found out his language was different from those of the natives.

"¿*Donde estamos*?" they studied their faces.

"¿*Como se llama este lugar*?" inquired another pointing at the ground.

"Sugbo," finally one of the gee stringers understood.

Each one of the men heard something differently. One perceived it was *Sebo*, another *Sebu* and the third Zebu. Whatever it was the scribe at the galleon wrote the word *Cebu*. The name was never meant to be interpreted differently, but differences in culture, language and idiosyncrasies prevented it from being so correctly. Besides, in Spanish *sebo* meant the fat of an animal, which was what the men were thinking incorrectly at that time, with the *lechon* roasting before them.

"*Tengo hambre*," one of them joked he was hungry and wanted to try a bite.

"Look, they are offering us to take a bite of the roasted pig!" said the guide.

Each one of them took a bite of the meat. They were also offered to drink their red coconut wine to down it with. After having tasted the crispy reddish pork skin and drank their wine, they thanked the four natives wholeheartedly. They went back to the ships and reported what they had found to the commander: that it was safe to anchor, the people were friendly and that plenty of food was in for the taking. They could stay for several days and haul in provisions for the onward voyage to their final destination.

CHAPTER 51

Their presence spread by word of mouth among the Sugboanons, then flew across the sea to Ilang-ilang's household in Opon like wild fire.

"I heard some men from far away are in Sugbo," said Nabilah.

"Yes, they are ," responded the young Ilang-ilang who only just arrived from her cousins in Sugbo.

"How do they look like?" questioned Asma who was recollecting all the plates after dinner, curious as she was.

"To tell you the truth, I haven't seen them yet. People who had seen them said they glowed under the sun."

"Huh, strange," commented Asma.

"These people must be exaggerating," responded Nabilah, with a practical understanding of the talk going on around town.

"Well, some credulous people from the villages said they might be *Ginoos*."

"Gods? I might not believe that," said Asma shaking her head in disagreement. "That remains to be verified."

"I've seen their ships. They were extremely huge, Asma . . . four ships, far away into the sea."

"What must they be up to?" questioned Nabilah , now taking a rest after a day's work.

Ilang-ilang was quick to say, "they must be lost or they must be into some kind of trouble."

". . . . perhaps. Who knows?"

"*Tata* would never trust them."

After wiping the table, Asma dried all the utensils and plates then made a comment in her usual low voice, "he is distrustful to anybody, how much more for some strange looking people from the high seas."

As always *Nabilah was* quick to defend her benefactor and warned her daughter, "I understand how he feels and Asma I want you to show some respect to the Datu."

"I hope they are friendly or we might have trouble ahead," Asma was quick to respond.

"They are hungry and I think they needed food and water. They couldn't afford to be bellicose or our men would eliminate them right away."

"In order to get food and water they should be friendly."

"I think the Rajah is under negotiations with them to land."

"Well, he is the Rajah and he can decide for the people."

"As far as I heard they are exchanging presents to tie friendship. My uncle received a box from them," Ilang-ilang continued.

"That must be because they wanted to land."

"Yeah . . ."

"What's inside the box?"

"I haven't seen it yet, but they say it was precious."

"Your *Tata* is against such show of artificial friendship. He said trusting strangers was a big blunder. They may look friendly but could only be putting up a front because they need something from us. Behind lurk some diabolic designs hidden in their show of friendship," concluded *Nabilah*.

CHAPTER 52

The sun was up on that eventful day of March 1521. High noon and the heat was unbearable. The Commander, after receiving the report of the advance party, decided to disembark and set foot personally on the shores of Sugbo for the first time. He brought with him silk cloth, flaxen wax, and so many things to establish friendship.

Not long after, free movements with the natives were seen in the streets all over the village. They roamed around shops, at the park and everywhere. They mingled with them. Closed to where the galleons were docked, was a large market. The proximity was a welcomed facility for the kitchen crew to easily haul in food and water.

Daniel and Jonas got off and mixed with the people at the market. It was bursting with activities, their eyes roamed to savor exotic things. All things were new to their senses. They couldn't believe their eyes to see different colorful tropical fruits displayed all over the market in stalls. All of them they wanted to take a bite and savor the freshness in them, to slurp the sweet meaty juice they had never ever tasted in their tables before. Months of sea travel without fruits or even food their tastes reached to a higher level of craving to try everything new at the same time. After trying one fruit after the other, they found out that mangoes were the best. They were juicy, tender and sweet.

It was the creaking of wheels from a cart which distracted their attention from the fruits. It wanted to wiggle its way among the baskets of fruits, meat and vegetable stalls, milling marketers, barterers and traders, so they moved sideways and let it pass. A smiling face met them, from a boy, sweat dripping from his brow, who was behind pushing it as hard as he could. Daniel thought the cart was too big for him to maneuver, dumbstruck as to how he did it. He was delivering melons, mangoes, bananas, coco, and guavas which were piled on top of each other jumbled into the cart, which rose high above his head.

They snaked their way through, passing several stalls until they stopped at a mango fruit stand. Mangoes were neatly stacked covering the whole stand from top to bottom resembling a football grandstand it was difficult to see where the stall attendant was. A small stocky man came out from behind and showed his yellowish teeth to them smiling.

"Mangoes?" he haggled with them.

"*Si*," Daniel was quick to say yes in a friendly way.

"How many do you like?" he retorted with a question, in his own dialect, by using his fingers to deliver his message.

"The whole basket."

Jonas couldn't remember how the transaction was done but it was concluded in a short time. Currency of any denomination was non-existent. Money to buy what they wanted was unheard of, not even the *ducats* which they brought with them had some value. They could only barter or exchange something for food, haggling as much as they could. In one stall, he had observed a young girl who was haggling for her charcoal for two pieces of fish, in another fruits for meat. They easily learned to trade this way, exchanging things for food. He took out his knife and offered it to the stall attendant who examined it, running his fingers on the surface to feel the Toledo *mark*, and the transaction was closed as easily as it was transacted.

They went further inward.

"Look almost all the stalls display only charcoal."

"How strange!" commented Daniel.

"What do you do with them," he dared to ask one of the stall owners.

"I think they use them for cooking," Daniel made it up, seeing that there was no reply from the man.

"Cooking?" Jonas eyebrows winced.

"Yes . . . imagine cooking three times a day, so there should be plenty of demand. They also use it for ironing."

"Charcoal . . . hmm. In Seville we call them carbon. Because of the so many carbons around, we might fittingly as well call this place *Carbon Market*. Yes . . . that name sounds appropriate."

They wandered around, wondering if there was anything they could barter as a souvenir, something tangible that they could bring home, aside from food. They approached one stall where kitchen utensils were displayed. They were looking at some locally crafted knives, when a long shadow hovered above the display. Jonas traced it and his eyes landed on a lovely native girl passing by apparently to do some bartering herself. She was tall, long legged and gorgeous. He couldn't help looking at her at the corner of his eyes. She was strikingly different from the other girls he had ever seen so far in his entire life, suddenly he was in love. It was as simple as that. Their eyes met and Jonas managed a cute smile. She acknowledged with a nod of her head and proceeded to a meat stall to do some bartering, two young maid escorts following behind. When she finished her transaction she transferred to another stall, then to another, and in the thick of the crowd she was gone, leaving both young lads in a spell.

"She was a pretty sight, wasn't she?" Daniel teased Jonas with an obvious question.

"Indeed she was. Now I found my souvenir, Daniel," he responded, still in a trance.

"Who was that girl?" Jonas questioned one stall attendant.

"Ilang-ilang," the girl watching one vegetable stall answered proudly.

"She was princess Ilang-ilang, the only daughter of the chieftain of Opon, a small island across the sea from Sugbo. Her father was the feared Datu, a great warrior and a relative of the Rajah of Sugbo!" the girl explained in her own dialect.

Upon hearing this, Jonas moved quickly after her but the thickness of the crowd prevented him from edging forward. He strained his eyes and craned his neck to look for her but she was gone like smoke that had come and gone. She seemed to be an illusion, a part of his imagination.

Lying in his cot that night, Jonas couldn't stop thinking of that girl's smile, her long legs and the way she swayed her hips when she walked away. Sexy and curvaceous in her sarong, she had whopping eyes and lush sensual lips. His heart thumped at the thought of her. His new found souvenir, his princess, his Ilang-ilang. As soon as they finished work the following day, Daniel invited Jonas to go downtown.

"Let's go down to the Carbon market and barter some citrus food, Jonas. We need to have plenty in stock for our onward journey," said Daniel. "I have some hand-over or second hands from a patient who died of scurvy, we could use them to barter for mangoes."

"Who knows we might see that girl again today, then I'd be bartering for my souvenir. Let's go then," Jonas kidded, to brighten up the day.

CHAPTER 53

The presence of the galleons spread by word of mouth across the land, reaching as far as many islands. Overnight Sugbo had been converted into a more interesting place to visit than any other, thanks to the people's credulity. And folks from the neighboring villages came merely to see them to satisfy their curiosity, of who they were and how they looked, taking special interest in their renowned immortality. These poor village people erroneously believed the tall white strangers from nowhere were *Ginoos*, the Gods they feared and revered all their life. And the rumor spread so fast, they trekked into Sugbo thinking it was an opportunity for a lifetime to see *Ginoos* in person.

It was also an opportunity for those who were entrepreneurial in spirit. Stalls bartering food opened everywhere, duplicating Sunday marketing in grand scale celebrated every day. People milled, chat and went to and fro.

It didn't last long though. On that one unfortunate sunny day, far away from where the hurly-burly was, an unforeseen incident happened. It's about three soldiers who strayed away from the group and roamed the peripheries of Sugbo in search of the most coveted mango. They were told at the market these fruits grew wildly on trees.

Inadvertently they violated the restriction to look for its source, ingenuously hoping to take more of them to the galleons and store some good fruits rich in vitamin C. They penetrated deeper into the woods where they found a river. There, along the banks of this river they found the mango trees. Like gold hanging on their branches the fruits sparkled under the sun, tempting to be picked.

At once they took off their heavy armors, climbed the trees and started picking them one by one. One of the men inched farther towards the other branches, in order to pick some more. Without realizing it they were beyond his reach. He was stocky and heavy and the branches sagged. A crack was heard and he fell into the side of the river. He rolled over and tumbled into the waters, his head hitting a big rock and fell unconscious. Blood spilled over. Obviously the branch he was hanging onto gave way due to his weight. The two others took no time to go down from their trees, but they were already too late. Ricardo died on the spot with hemorrhage. In the afternoon his body was retrieved and sent to the galleons.

The false belief in their immortality soon found an awful end. It would have remained undiscovered had it not been for this tragic fiasco which happened most unfortunately. They weren't immortals after all. The natives learned of the deception by default. *Ginoos* would never die, concluded those who had believed them to be so. They were as human as anybody else, prone to bodily harm and death. The story spread as fast as virus all throughout the village, thereby breaking the spell of their immortality.

In due course, people got back into believing in their superhuman *Ginoos* and trekked back to where they came from, disillusioned at what they had thought was a miracle from heaven.

Baguio, Linug and *Baha* made the center stage again. *Baguio*, the most ferocious brought strong winds and rain, and blew nipa huts down whenever he got angry. *Linug* ate up houses, bringing them down into the center of the earth whenever he trembled. *Baha* was the lesser of the Gods, destroying only crops when he flooded the rivers.

"What a deception," said Akmal.

"Exactly what I had told you all along," hissed the Datu, confirming his belief.

"It was some people's fault in believing them so," said Yaya Nabilah in defense of the sea people.

"They're still to be blamed. If they didn't look differently mistakes would have been avoided."

"But they didn't do anything to deceive! Their appearances might be deceiving but if they didn't act deceptively there won't be any deceptions. It's actions that make it deceitful," interrupted *ibu*, who was listening at the sides for some time.

"Preposterous!" *ayah*'s voice grew loud.

"*Ibu* is right, *ayah*," Ilang-ilang couldn't bear herself to comment seeing her mother's logic.

"Enough of this nonsense! Still I don't see any reason that I should go and meet them at the feast. Do you remember when that tribe from the north came setting fire to our houses? Ilang-ilang, you know what to tell your uncle. Tell him not to expect my presence."

CHAPTER 54

Daniel and Jonas shaved, cut their hair short and made themselves look human. After taking a refreshing dip in the sea, they strolled around the village, hoping to find some souvenirs. Some of the stalls folded up for the day. They had had enough. Those which were still opened were food stalls whose owners were hoping to have a last ditch for their perishables. Hanging in most of these food stalls were yellow coco leaves woven into heart shaped receptacles which definitely contained food. Strange, they thought.

"*¿Cual son?*" Daniel was curious of what they were.

"*Pusó*," said one stall owner smiling.

In their curiosity they cut one in half and saw that it was rice inside, white as the sky tainted by a shade of yellow, from the coco leaves. Back in Seville Jonas remembered a Chinese who once told him that there were a hundred ways of preparing rice. You could have it with tomato sauce, rice cooked in bamboos, wrapped in banana leaves, cooked in charcoal, in a pot or just plain rice. And then there's *paella*, Shanghai rice, Indian rice, so on and so forth, he didn't have any ideas what they were.

Two entirely unique individuals from two different spectrums, personalities from different angles and dimensions who were meant to converge at a common point in time and place, to give meaning into each other's lives. Destiny would have been different if the King of Spain had not been interested in financially supporting the voyage. Their fate would have gone in a different direction if Jonas hadn't made it to the galleons. He wouldn't have found the princess of his dreams.

Meanwhile his Ilang-ilang was out there doing the usual things she was doing. It took an hour to cross the sea from her island to Sugbo, and she only came when she had to go to the market or visit her cousins where life was never dull. Even ordinary people crossed this short trip every day to get their supplies which were not readily available in her place, especially things new and trendy which came ahead for a month. His heart virtually ached with an overwhelming feeling of the most profound longing to see her again. Today not even her shadow appeared and Jonas missed her.

Ilang-ilang, his newly found princess was about five feet and four inches tall, with a slim figure and legs that matched her entire body proportionally. She exuded charm in a perfectly healthy body with a well-defined waist that curved downward in a womanly fashion. It was easy to understand why they knew her at the market. Aside from being a princess she also possessed a friendly disposition. Her long thick black hair that dangled up to her shoulder that shone under the light of the sun, flew like feathers when she walked. Set proportionally apart, under thick curving brows she had twinkling eyes which were soft and alluring, and a skin as tan as a light auburn color, undoubtedly due to her Asian ancestry. Ilang-ilang was different. Not even the girls back in Seville had touched his heart so profoundly. It was the uniqueness of the place and the exotic combination of her beauty that Jonas was captivated so easily. It was love at first sight.

CHAPTER 55

It was Saturday evening and guests started pouring in. The mini palace was worthy of its being called a palace, huge an edifice as it was which stood conspicuously in the midst of the smaller huts in the village. The Sugboanons were proud of its existence as if it was their own, like a public building owned collectively by everybody. The architecture itself was uniquely royal, in the style of the Malay buildings found everywhere: the roofs sloped down at the sides forming a pyramid, then looped upwards to form rain stoppers which conduct water to gutters; twelve pillars stood in symmetry along the walls to hold these roofs up constructed purposely for air ventilation; the walls were covered with rattan frames woven closely to form panels placed uniformly side by side; six large windows adorned with silk drapes kept rains out during rainy days; there was a flight of stairs that went up to a massive door that stood in the middle. It was opened tonight and elegant men and women streamed-in one by one.

Prominent men and women of Sugbo graced the occasion with their lovely evening outfits. Among the local guests was Ilang-ilang who came in earlier invited by her two cousins, daughters of the Rajah. She was dressed to the occasion and glittered strikingly with her new flowing dress, which displayed her true sensuous beauty. She was seated at one table with them. Men, women, young Couples, and tribe leaders with their wives came streaming in, smiling and greeting each other at the entrance. Some waited at the promenade for their companions, at the door and some strode inside to find their respective seats.

The hall began to swell up with guests in pairs, husbands and wives, partners and friends. They chatted around tables arranged equally on both sides of the hall. Dayang and Dana, the two daughters of Rajah were seated with Ilang-ilang in one of the tables. Food and drinks were laid on a long table at the center. Most conversations were centered on the galleon people and their infamous discredited immortality.

"Do you think they are similar to us?" Dana commented innocently.

"I don't think so . . . they're so colorless, so pale," joked Dayang inoffensively.

"And look at the abundant hair on their arms and faces."

"Some innocent village people had been led to believe they were *Ginoos*. If it were not for that fatal incident at the river some people would still have believed them to be so and they would have maintained the big lie until now," stated Dana as if she personally knew the fact.

"With all due respect, who led them to believe so? At home, we had the same argument. *Nana* and Yaya think it would be unfair to judge these people without any basis at all." Ilang-ilang came in defense against the rumors going around.

"*Ginoos* make strange phenomena, they do things we humans can't. Look at *Linug*. When he strikes the earth shakes, he brings everything down to the earth," retorted Dana.

"Right," commented Dana.

"And it seems they only have one sex . . . only male. Have you seen anyone like us, females among them," added Dana mischievously.

The two girls giggled at Dana's comment.

Daniel and Jonas were among those lucky ones chosen to come. They had been handpicked by the captain due to exemplary conduct. Together with the commander, the other acting captains of the surviving galleons and some other officials, all of them dressed down to the occasion in white formal military uniform , marched towards the mini palace.

When the commander's group came in through the massive door, the talking and noise subsided. All attention was diverted to them while they marched towards the Rajah to pay respect. Jonas noticed guards with spears standing at both sides of the door. He surveyed the interior with a keen eye, figuring out the room arrangements and admiring the ornaments hanging on the walls, seeing it had a traditional Malay layout. This spacious room, the hall, must be where all celebrations and important functions were held, he speculated silently. Daniel had similar impressions. The lighting was subdued and soft to the eyes.

"*Buenas noches, Señor,*" greeted the commander, respectfully with a bow.

The Rajah did the same by tilting his head a little to acknowledge. Exchange of gifts followed then all of them were led to their seats, the commander and the four captains seated themselves closed to the Rajah and his entourage of followers.

As they were seated Jonas stopped surveying the place. He had a feeling he would see the girl at the market here in this most likely occasion of important people in Sugbo. He scanned the faces of all those present, from left to right, table by table. He saw unfamiliar faces of men and women wearing *sarongs* and multi colored turbans on their heads, they didn't mean anything to him. It didn't take him long to find her though. His heart skipped a bit when at the side of his eyes he recognized her familiar feature sitting at one table with two other girls.

She had taken notice of him first when they came in. Ilang-ilang thought he looked elegantly tall with that white uniform the military used to wear in formal occasions. If she knew it was borrowed more likely she would have bickered and laughed at the thought. Jonas was tickled at the thought.

"That's the one I saw at the market, Dayang," Ilang-ilang whispered to Dayang, making reference to Jonas.

"The one on the left? Well, he's handsome!" Dayang whispered.

" Yeah, but too fresh and aggressive, winking at me."

"He must have liked you, Ilang-ilang. A crush at first sight, " Dana interrupted naughtily.

The banquet was highlighted by the introduction of the guests, which the Rajah smartly maneuvered with all diplomatic decorum. Names of the guest were called one by one and each one recognized the introduction by standing up or bowing. When Ilang-ilang's turn came, she stood up and made a curtsy.

"So, Ilang-ilang's her name... And she's now without any trace of doubt a princess. What the girl at the market said was true," Jonas muttered to himself.

Daniel elbowed him. "Now you see why she's different."

"That makes it more exciting. I would then pretend myself as the prince with the shining armor," Daniel smiled at Jonas' comment. But he was serious.

"You're dreaming again, Jonas. How would you do that? Remember our stay is limited to a couple of days." Daniel was right but Jonas believed love knows no bounds, no barriers, no language nor race.

Drinks were served around by beautiful young attendants on wooden trays. All of them were amazed at the exotic beauty of this island, including Daniel who could not contain himself from admiring.

Jonas' eyes stopped loitering and now were focused at the Rajah, and occasionally to no other than Ilang-ilang. He didn't want to miss any of her movements so he kept on glancing sideways to her direction. She became conscious. She stood to reach for a glass her movements calculatingly dainty and flawless which never escaped the observant eyes of people. Jonas couldn't help glancing her way and admiring silently. He wanted to be near her, to touch her, and to feel her to see if she was real. And to tell her how much he admired her beauty. She was astoundingly beautiful beyond his imagination. When she got back to her seat, she glanced his way and caught him looking at her with the same smile. Jonas looked away pretending not to be looking, but Ilang-ilang got the message alright. She thought he was too daring and aggressive.

"If he would only stop staring at me," she thought. But it didn't stop. Jonas couldn't stop glancing at her. And the more she felt conscious the more he was pestering her with his glances.

"Who does he think he is ?" she felt awkward and also couldn't stop taking stolen glimpses at him, every glimpse giving her some insights into his well designed face, from angle to angle, tip to tip, which was now slowly getting clearer. "Well, he isn't ugly at all with eyes as blue as the sky. Only he is a stranger and who knows where he came from?"

"Why not," Jonas reflected. "Why not bring her with me back to Seville to be my souvenir? It would not be a bad idea, after all."

Jonas looked at his glass, took a sip, then raised it to the girls and pronounced "cheers", in his clear Spanish southern accent. At that distance he could sense they were giggling and whispering to each other.

CHAPTER 56

Dinner was served and the feasting began. Food was plenty and extravagant while drinks kept coming non-stop. The Rajah, the Commander and the captains discussed politics, the route to *Maluku* island and issues only men would delve into, such as the conversion of the people to Christianity. They talked on and on.

Daniel and Jonas got up, walked across the hall and joined the girls who were also delighted to have them as company.

"Can we have the pleasure of sitting with you lovely girls?" Jonas volunteered, expecting no immediate replies. He wondered if they understood.

"By all means," said Dayang in her dialect, who was at the same time directing them to sit with them around the table, moving sideways to give spaces for two more chairs. Then one servant came snappily to insert two chairs.

"*Gracias,*" they said in unison when the servant left, bowing his head. They took their seats gladly, apprehensive of what actions to take.

"*¿Como se llama ella?*" explored Daniel who was pointing to the girl on the right.

"Dayang," volunteered Dana, to break the ice. Dayang and Dana could be taken as twins. They had the same dress color, style and even mannerisms.

"*Soy Jonas y mi amigo, Daniel,*" he pointed at himself then to his friend to introduce themselves, aware of the eyes of envious people from the sides.

This was followed by Dana introducing herself and Ilang-ilang, who were amused at hearing the sound of the new language. Jonas seated himself beside Ilang-ilang and their legs touched, sending him a feeling of interminable euphoria. He was entranced by her beauty and charm. The closer he was the more he was enchanted. She was indeed real.

Slowly he was falling for her strikingly simple ways, which was quite disarming; he even almost forgot where he came from- that he was only a poor stowaway who was able to get food by working at the kitchen. Strange how life changed because of some unanticipated intervening events, this one the best ever that happened to him, to be in a strange far away land and serendipitously found the princess of his life. Their glances met. He sensed that she began to be fond of him as well.

"Would it be possible to fall for a foreigner in spite of so many differences in culture and language and the impossibility of my father's consenting to such a weird relationship?" Ilang-ilang shook her head unconsciously.

Jonas thought that perhaps it was his sleekness in that white military uniform he was wearing and the uniqueness of his being a foreigner which softened her impression towards him. If she only knew the uniform was loaned, but still in spite of this small insignificant factor he nevertheless stood out among the rest of the group, except his friend, Daniel, who was also good looking. When Jonas moved he could sense the two sisters whispering something to Ilang-ilang.

"Your glass is empty. Would you like some more of that," she said, offering him another fill. A pretty servant girl with a tray passed by, Ilang-ilang lifted one glass and offered it to him.

"*Gracias*," Jonas said thank you.

"*Gracias*?" she repeated with eyes wide open.

The night seemed to fly so fast. The talk went on and on. The issues flew to serious topics such as Christianity, herself, his life, Sugbo, her beliefs and his beliefs, most importantly Spanish and her language, almost all the time lost in translation, so ever aware of their differences, yet conscious of the attraction that they had for each other.

"I think perhaps we should fill up our glasses," she suggested decisively with a slight gesture of her hand with the glass.

Jonas obliged and got up, collected their empty glasses and followed her into a little connecting room, leaving Daniel, Dana and Dayang behind. The lights were low and a divinely laid table with a hand-woven white mantle revealed itself. Music was all over the place. There at the center was the same mysterious oak box which had bothered him for so long. He was struck by the little coincidence. So, this was where it ended. How easy it was to learn its content without the risks of being caught empty handed at his uncle's cabin. It was already opened in front and the content was exposed for everybody to see. It was a small image of the Santo Niño. He felt a sense of awe and reverence; it radiated a reddish iridescent glow before his eyes. Automatically, he made a sign of the cross, his attention trapped for a brief second, he almost forgot she was beside him.

"It was a gift from your people," she commented, shaking him from his trance.

"I'm sorry," Jonas said, after he sprang back to his own self.

He switched back to her. She had filled up their glasses and extended one to him. He drew himself closer and caught her hand with the glass. A look of embarrassment was etched across her face by the unexpected sudden touch. Her response was to smile at his advances but withdrew her hand shyly. Then she suggested they return to their seats with the group.

"Tomorrow is Sunday. What do you usually do on Sundays," Jonas dared to take a bolder step.

"Sometimes I come here to visit my cousins. Most of the time I stayed in Opon," she timidly found her words, her eyes at her glass.

"Do you have anything planned tomorrow?"
She bit her lips, and at the back of her mind she was checking her schedule.

"I'm free tomorrow. I thought that we could go for a walk somewhere together...and you show me the countryside," he volunteered, too aggressively perhaps. But she didn't flinched at all.

Meanwhile, Daniel was enjoying the company of Dana and Dayang, who were trying to learn the language and for him to learn theirs. They taught themselves the numbers first then followed by the common expressions. This went on and on, he was wondering if they would ever remember everything, even at school these were learned for years and students never got them perfectly, how much more for a one night lesson?

"I was planning to come to Sugbo to see my grandmother who lives alone in one of those hills."

"Is she expecting you?"

"Yes, she is."

"Would it be a crowd if I'd come with you?"

She smiled. She took another sip of her drink and looked at him in the eye without saying anything.

The night was getting to a close, the merrymaking and drinking went on it seemed never to end at all. Jonas never wanted it to end at all. Wives were tired and bored they urged their husbands to go home. Then a sudden surge of wind came in through the windows. Jonas noticed the glasses were moving, for a second he considered it was caused by the wind. Then the lights went out and somebody shouted *"Linug"*. They heard the crashing of plates and glasses as they fell on the marbled floor, this time Jonas was so sure it was an earthquake, his instincts told him to duck his head. In the middle of darkness he crept rapidly under a table, remembering what his father had told him when something like this happens.

Knowing their way in darkness, Dayang and Dana rushed outside, not realizing they left Ilang-ilang behind. They wanted to go back but it was unsafe for them to go inside with all the falling debris. Daniel also made a rush outside at the first tremor.

Ilang-ilang did what Jonas had done. Instincts told her that it was safer to go under the table than to run outside in the dark, when everybody run about chaotically, not knowing where to go. When the second tremor came she heard more crashing and tumbling of things around so she crouched even more. Jonas felt her presence and greeted her, "hello".

It was a situation more embarrassing for Ilang-ilang, who had never had a fast encounter as this one before her, than to him. Then a third tremor struck, this time stronger. She moved herself closer. Jonas held her hand tightly to instill the assurance she needed. She didn't withdraw nor pulled it away this time. For him it was eternal. They both listened closely looking for exits or any light that could lead the way. When he was assured it was clear, they ran as fast as they could, still holding hands towards the moonlight that led them outside.

It was a blessing, without which would have been impossible for Jonas to establish the bond he had so much desired with Ilang-ilang. He knew there were obstacles. Time was short. As soon as the loading of the provisions were done the galleons would have to continue the voyage to *Maluku* island. There was also her father who was ever wary and distrustful of foreigners.

CHAPTER 57

When she reached home after the feast her father was at the door waiting for her. The earthquake must have worried him so much that her presence was necessary to put him at ease. Her mother was also worried. Ilang-ilang expected them to give her a hug, to tell her they were happy she was safe and home at last. But what welcomed her was a cold reception from her father. He was direct and blunt in his first question.

"Ilang-ilang, I hope you got something from the feast?"

This did not as much surprise her, knowing her father's animosity towards the visitors. She had anticipated that he would confront her by the time she reached home and she was prepared for her answers.

"I did get something, *Tata*," she gloated. " I've learned so many things. These people are similar to us. They are as human as the people of Sugbo and Opon."

He looked at her with raised eyebrow. "They are different. They look different and speak a different tongue," his tone raised a scale on hearing her impertinence.

Ilang-ilang launched her defense with a low voice, ever so respectful. "That doesn't make any difference because they are humans. In fact their language sounds musical."

She thought of Jonas , his sad eyes and his soft caring ways. He could never be different.

"Huh! I hope you won't see them again. I forbid you to see any one of them."

"But *Tata*, it's illogical and unfair," she insisted further.

"I know... one of your escorts told me you were having an exceptionally intimate conversation with one of them."

"But it was normal to receive them, being the Rajah's guests."

"Bah! Your uncle is too soft on them. Giving a feast for nothing? If I were the Rajah I would have driven them back to the sea..."

"... and one more thing. I forbid you to see your cousins while these people are still here in Sugbo."

Before she could complain her mother came out from the bedroom where she was all the time listening.

"Did the earthquake destroy the palace," interrupted *nana* when she could not bear to listen to their repartees.

"They would have to do some repairs especially with the roof which fell down."

"And casualties?"

"I couldn't be more at ease if there were. Luckily *Linug* was compassionate. His strength was not as strong enough to take some people with him."

"Every now and then *Linug* comes, Ilang-ilang, sometimes weak and most of the time dreadfully strong. Yes, Sugbo is well protected... from the great winds... never from *Linug*,"

"You're still up, nana?"

"I have been waiting for you to be home, my mind was out there with you in Sugbo. I'm glad you're home."

"I'm old enough to take care of myself, *Nana*."

"Go to bed now," her *Tata* interrupted.

"Goodnight, *Tata*. Good night *Nana*."

Ilang-ilang went to bed with her mind on Jonas. "What is he doing now?" she couldn't brush his face off from her mind. "I had misjudged him from the beginning. I should never have trusted my first impression," she thought. His voice kept ringing in her ears, his blue eyes penetrating. For the first time in her life she had met someone who was so intriguing and impressive as Jonas. But she couldn't see him anymore. Her father made it clear. On the other hand, something inside her was telling her to see him again. Who should she follow? If she followed her father's orders she would not see him anymore and her heart would ache for the rest of her days. It would be painful but the pain would go away as soon as they leave Sugbo, but she was unsure if she could bear the pain . She had to decide and this decision would come from her heart .

Ilang-ilang couldn't help thinking about Jonas. In the few days after the feast she kept recalling something about the encounter, the light touch of the hands, the look in his eyes and everything about him. The undefined emotions that Jonas aroused in her, which she had thought was a dream, and never existed.

Now she opened her eyes and a new feeling of uncertainty confounded her, inexperienced as she was with a first love , the total resistance of her father against strangers complicated everything.

CHAPTER 58

Back at the galleons there was singing among those who were left behind. Men got into music as an outlet, to lighten the weight and soften the hearts that grew tough due to hardships. Jonas' mind was still whirling after that feast. There was singing but his heart was left back in that mini-palace.

"*Según ellos, yo no soy digno de ser dueño de tu amor....*"

"You sing so well Luis," Jonas heard Daniel commenting after the song.

"Thank you."

"You are not only a champion chess player but also a good singer."

"I wanted to be a singer, but there's no future in singing, you end up singing in the streets. Look at them they are all beggars."

"I truthfully admire people who could sing. And where did you learn your guitar playing?" Daniel was curious.

"I learned it by myself."

"Honestly . . . but how? I wanted to learn it myself, but it hurts my fingers."

"I listened to songs, and then tickle my guitar one string at a time until I got the correct tune. My father gave me my first guitar when I was five and since then I had been playing."

"Can you teach me how?"

"It needs patience. I know you have plenty of that. And your fingers... don't worry about the pain. Soon you won't feel it anymore."

"My favourite songs are the boleros. What's yours?"

"I love `The Poem of the Cid´."

"Can you sing that for me, please?" Daniel requested.

Silence permeated the air. He strummed the guitar and started singing.

> *"Con sus ojos muy grandemente llorando*
> *tornaba la cabeza y estaba los mirando:*
> *vio las puertas abiertas, los postigos sin candado,*
> *las perchas vacías sin pieles y sin mantos*
> *y sin halcones y sin azores mudados.*
> *Suspiró mío Cid triste y apesadumbrado.*
> *Habló mío Cid y dijo resignado:*
> *¡Loor a ti, señor Padre, que estás en lo alto!*
> *Esto me han urdido mis enemigos malos . . . "*

When Luis ended his singing everybody in the galleon clapped their hands in appreciation. They thought he was the best. His rich and splendid voice echoed in the air, by which in the stillness of the night, drifted the merry sound of the ballad.

They heard Luis sing at night, in the mornings and in the afternoons; anywhere he went his music echoed. It was alleviating. It lifted every body's heart, Jonas' most especially

In his cot Jonas was thinking of Ilang-ilang, still overwhelmed by the emotions of the night, and was overjoyed by his discovery. She was totally different from other girls. That was the first time he realized he loved her. He loved how she looks at him, how she smiles and listens when he spoke as if she was enthralled by his language. He loved how she walks, her black hair and everything in her. He couldn't stop thinking about her.

On his back he lay dreaming, staring up the ceiling wide awake into the night. He wondered about all the possibilities of how he could bring her with him.

Now his focus was Ilang-ilang wherever he went, whatever he was doing. The image of her face flashed before his eyes, her voice echoed clearly in his head. She was all over him. He was always imagining how he would kiss her, held her and touch her. Since their encounter nothing entered his mind but his souvenir, his princess.

CHAPTER 59

Linug was the reason, the bridge of all this wonderful friendship and the beginning of something unexpectedly wonderful which eventually would turn into an everlasting bond. They saw each other on that Sunday in spite of all the odds, difference in culture and the language barrier, at her grandmother's. The sun was beyond the clear blue sky, partly covered by thin white foamy clouds.

"Your grandmother was a joy to be with. Does she live alone?" Jonas was curious.

"Yes. My *nana* always insisted she must have somebody with her or live with us at home where there are many useful hands who could take care of her. She's only eighty three and she runs around the house to do everything for herself. She said she'd rather be alone than have somebody whom she couldn't get along with. I think she was affected seriously by my *nana*'s running away with my *tata*."

"I wouldn't be surprised if she'd lived up to more than a hundred, with that vitality of hers."

They saw each other again and again on the few days following that Sunday. Time was short and the more they thought of it the more they missed each other. Their favorite meeting place was under a mango tree at the top of the hill overlooking Sugbo, near her grandmother's thatched house where the view was breathtaking. After seeing her grandmother they would spread mantel piece on the shade, where they sat and talk the whole day about almost everything, savoring every single moment together, wrapped in each other's arms and far away from the scrutinizing critical eyes of her people.

"I have another grandmother, actually my great grandmother, Hana, who's already about a hundred years old. Our family live very long, Jonas. Someday you'll meet her, too. There was a story about her. It was her love story. She was abducted and taken to the woods. Lore has it that my great-grandfather fought and killed her abductors single handedly to rescue her. He was one of the strongest in Sandakan and folks thought he had an *anting-anting.*"

"What's an *anting-anting*?"

"Well, it's an amulet which had made him strong and invincible. It's a protection."

"Can it make a person invisible?"

"Why do you want to do that? So that you could do whatever you want to do to take advantage of invisibility?"

Obviously kidding, he whispered, "Well, it's a protection, you said. And I want some of it. Besides I want to be invisible from you and from other people, so that when I want to see you, when I miss you, I could merely disappear and at the click of my fingers be right there in your very midst, any time I want to."

"Ridiculous," she pinched him at the sides where it tickled so much.

Seeing each other every day required her to come to the mainland without her father's knowledge by taking the one hour boat trips. She was completely resolved her love was worth more than anything else in the world, and she was ready to risk all of it even to the point of going against the wishes of her father. She was determined to leave all of it, her people, her culture and her birthplace for Jonas.

It didn't take long for these frequent trips to come to her father's knowledge. He was furious and forbade her from seeing Jonas further. In spite of the prohibition Ilang-ilang continued to see him by escaping, her bodyguards and maids were no match to her excuses. Love had demonstrated to be stronger still, in spite of all the odds.

Teaching her Spanish wasn't too difficult at all. First words, followed with simple sentences, subject and predicate, then nouns with verbs until they understood each other. Ilang-ilang was intelligent and zealous in absorbing so many words in his language. This made him love her more.

"*Mi amor, te adoro muchisimo.* Let me think of a way. Your father's objection makes me more determined than ever to go with it through."

"I love you, too, Jonas."

"Do you know of any place we could go to and hide ourselves?"

"Oh, Jonas, I'm so afraid."

"Seville is on the other side of the world, it took us two years to come here. I have a country house, with my papa and mama who would be more than willing to keep us for as long as we want. We could plant vegetables and raise animals. Anything I would do , *cariño* , as long as we are together."

"I would come with you where ever you want us to go, my love."

"I don't want to lose you, *cariño*."

"We have Sandakan to look forward to. My great-grandfather died recently, but I still have my great-grandma and some close relatives. If only a boat could take us there."

Jonas put his arms around her, kissed her tenderly, gently pressing his lips to hers, as if somehow feeling he wouldn't see her again, his head bent over hers, lips over hers, adoring her, and whispering "*Yo te amo.*"

"Oh, *cariño* . . ." Jonas was carried away by her sweet smell and warm lips, bewildered as he was, even so willing to give it all in the name of love.

Then she was reminded of her father who must already be mad. She was apprehensive and scared that he must be all over Sugbo now looking for her.

What if her people were against this relationship, too? So, the whole world was against it. The realization dawned on Ilang-ilang.

"If her father had judged against it, would her people be of the same opinion? What if the *Ginoos* were also against this relationship?" she asked with a heavy sigh, in her halting Spanish. Jonas assured her that it would not be so, and that they would come out of it triumphantly. He held her close and kissed her, thinking that if he could only hide her somewhere temporarily, to bring her with him to Spain when the right time comes, everything would come out all right. When would the right time be? He was hoping falsely against hope, and time was short when the galleons would be sailing in a few days' time.

CHAPTER 60

It was towards the end of their stay when they saw each other again in that afternoon. The hauling of provisions at the four galleons had come to an end. Jonas had a feeling that it might be for the last time. Soft winds were blowing lightly enough to cool the warm air from the sea. At the hilltops the panorama of the whole village was breathtakingly fascinating, they were enjoying every bit of it. Ilang-ilang who was acting as the perfect guide, was showing him all the places she was familiar with, telling him everything about Sugbo: the mini palace, carbon market, the main streets and beyond all this, the gleaming sea that divided the two islands. Farther out across she was proud to show her birthplace, Opon, which was jutted by small huts and coconut trees along the coastline. All this: the perfect setting, the timing, and their love, but she was completely not at ease. Something was amiss and out of place.

Jonas was oblivious of the dangers that lurked hidden somewhere, ready to jump on him at anytime. Indeed, somewhere out there a secret diabolic plan was hatched to put an end to their relationship.

"Find them. They should be somewhere in Sugbo."

"Sugbo is so big, Fakir."

"You can start with the Rajah's daughters. Pester them if you must. They should know."

"And as soon as we find them what should we do with him?"

"You know what to do, " said Fakir, one of the Datu's henchmen.

"Oo."

"The Datu's instructions are very clear. All you have to do is bring him here."

"What if he resists?"

"If he does then you can use force. But you should bring him here alive. Is that clear?"

"Oo," one of the men said yes in his dialect.

It was already getting dark when Jonas and Ilang-ilang got down from the hills. Suddenly, a strange feeling of danger came his way, similar to premonition. Panic set in. Mouth dry, He wanted to shout help, he couldn't. Run, but in which direction? His muscles suddenly turned weak.

"That's him," Jonas heard one of the men.

"No! Don't touch him, please! Fakir, please," Ilang-ilang virtually begged them, upon realizing what was happening.

Five men from hiding approached, and blocked their way without any questions. Surprised as he was his mind was blocked, he couldn't think which way to go anymore. They held him Immobile. Jonas wanted to resist but it was hard to overpower five men with weapons. They ganged up on him when he showed some resistance and tied both his hands. Unable to fight back he was dragged into some place, at the insistence and pleadings of Ilang-ilang. There were no explanations given.

Soon he found himself tied on a post in the middle of the plaza, weary and bruised, awaiting for a decision to be carried for his execution or release. Jonas thought he would die. He cried injustice, but there was no justice under the Datu who was the law, judge and the executioner. His words were above all else.

Ilang-ilang took everything calmly. When she got back to her composure she went straight to her father to plead for Jonas' release, but he was nowhere to be found, evidently hiding from her knowing that he would eventually give in to her supplications and entreaties. She went to the Rajah desperately for help, but the latter was also powerless, telling her of the impossibility of going against her people's wishes.

She was at a total loss. All those people whom she thought could help her had turned their backs on her. The least that she expected was Daniel, but he was her last resort. She was adamant that he might take it differently, too. In her desperation she went straight to him who was at the galleon. Ilang-ilang was shaking when she told the story.

"I loved him more than anything else. Please help me Daniel if there's anything that you can do to help him," she implored with all honesty.

"I told him he was treading on dangerous grounds. Oh poor Jonas, if only he had listened to my advice. He acted beyond reason, saying he would risk everything as long as you're together. He loves you, my dear. Have you seen your father for his sake?" inquired Daniel.

"I've been looking for him all over Sugbo and Opon. I know my father. He doesn't heed to reasons anymore, he judged all of you as a menace to our people," she was trembling. She knew her father's hatred of foreigners and he was brutal.

Daniel saw how powerless he was, not knowing what to do. He searched her further by asking, "Do you know where Jonas is now?"

Ilang-ilang was sobbing profusely and with trembling voice she said, "they had taken him, I don't know where. In all probability they'd put him at the center of town in Opon, in view for everybody else to see, like ordinary punishments to transgressors. There were five men who blocked our way and I knew instantly that they were my father's men."

"Let me think, my dear. I'll talk with some friends and see what we can do. For the meantime, promise me that you would stay here. Don't move until we get Jonas back to the galleon."

"I would. Please be in a hurry, Daniel."

CHAPTER 61

Daniel started with Luis and Jose at the kitchen. He told them about what's happening to their friend and asked them what they could do to save him. Soon the men at the galleons were stirred, worried as to what they were going to do to help. Some of Jonas' friends planned to do it on their own. But this reached the Commander who immediately called a meeting to organize a rescue operation, ordering skiffs to be equipped with sixty men to depart right away. If they had done it to recover the lost skiff, how much more would it be done necessarily in order to save one's life, justified his uncle, Juan Serrano. Weapons were checked and swords sharpened.

Daniel joined in. Leather snapped and steel clanged. He had put on his red breeches, yellow sleeves, red and yellow shoulder pads, then attached his leg and arm armors proud to have worn them finally. He could see his image on his well-polished steel corselet that shone like a mirror. He picked up his helmet and saw it fitted him well. Then he stood up from his cot to see how he looked. He then tied his laces after putting on his leather boots. His gauntlets were on his cot which he would use later on. Everybody in the team did the same including the Commander who was now ready for combat. At dawn the following day, 28th of April, six skiffs splashed onto the waters to sail towards Opon. All sixty well-equipped men, majority of whom, were Jonas' friends hopped eagerly onto their respective places.

Rowing at the distance, the small flickering yellow dotted lights along the shoreline were evident. Waves were lapping as they edge forward and the breeze whispered. Stomachs rumbled and grumbled. Some farted.

They were hoping the natives were still in their respective huts asleep, so that landing could be done surreptitiously and creeping inland easier. But landing to shore was impossible because the tide was low, so they had to embark at about a third of a league away and had to wade through knee-deep waters filled with sharp corals that made their pace slower. Eleven men stayed behind to watch the boats.

After the paddling and squelching, they reached the shoreline in the middle of dawn, when light was beginning to come out from the horizon. The sea air was a bit chilly. The rushing of the waves on the shore and the shuffling and crunching of their boots on the sand were frustratingly audible, however much careful they were to make so much noise. Waking up the natives was critical to the operation. One could sound the alarm for the whole village to come and take up arms against them.

They edged forward few steps at a time. Somewhere pigs snorted and snuffled. First was to locate his position. So they set their direction towards the center which was most likely a place for executions in the village. They were hoping their judgment were right. The sound of silence was maddening they heard only the occasional barking of native dogs somewhere in the distance, the clumping of their footsteps and the rattling of swords inside their scabbards.

It was not long to locate the center of Opon. Through a maze of small huts they jiggled their way and finally found the clearing. The commander ordered them to stop and study the surroundings before initiating their moves.

At the distance they could make out two men pacing in the wide clearing. They saw Jonas there alright, tied to a pole in the middle, head drooping. He was unconscious. Five guards armed with bamboo lances and bolos on their sides were taking turns to see that nobody came nearer. Three were lying asleep on a large bamboo *lantay* and the other two were pacing back and forth to keep themselves awake during their shift.

To overrun and subdue these five guards was not too difficult for fifty strong men. To keep them from waking the rest of the tribe was another thing. They would have to start eliminating the two who were on guard. Two arrows were needed to eliminate them first, so two of the best archers were ordered to do the first job. They swished directly on target, hitting one on the neck and one at the thorax sending them to fall on the ground at the same time. The other three who were still sleeping were easily eliminated as well.

Jonas' hands were untied as fast as they could then carried him on one's shoulder, as he was unconscious and wounded. He was badly beaten and his eyes were shot. They were glad he was still alive. Carrying him on one's shoulder was the only way they could do it but this hampered and slowed escape. He groaned unconsciously as they hefted him. They scurried away without wasting any time.

In one of those huts, some of those who were awake heard the creaking of leather, shuffling of feet, scrapping of boots and a jumble of unknown sounds they made on their retreat. One went out to inquire and saw the five lifeless guards on the ground. He sounded the alarm crying out as loud as he could, and woke everybody up. Men came out of their huts one by one. From their sleep it took them sometime to realize what was happening.

Dawn had broken earlier and the morning light saw the men already half way through running, the shore was already within reach in a few minutes. When he looked back Daniel saw hundreds of torches on their heels or maybe a thousand bolo brandishing natives who were running behind , eager to strike and pound on all of them. The archers downed those who were in the first line. There was shouting and howling of crazy men, snorting much the same as bulls on the attack to gorge anything on their way. Their distance became shorter and shorter until they were overran.

The first ones finally reached the shore then waded through the waters to their skiffs. Jonas was laid on the floor then the rest of the men turned back to help the last ones to confront the maddening crowd. They had to act fast or the angry pursuers would catch up on all of them. Close fighting began. There was clanging and clinking of steel, bolos against swords, bamboo against iron spears and bodies fell. Arrows flew and swished past them, some made thudding sounds on the sides of the skiffs. Daniel ducked.

The commander was one of the last to come. He was about to climb on the boat when he was hit by an arrow on the leg and fell on the water. He stood up to balance himself limping. The rest of the men came to his rescue but they were also held off by the raining arrows. More and more natives came closer and pounded on them. The rest of the men stayed with the Commander to fend off the subduing natives but the enemy's strength in number was too much for them to hold on.

Many of the natives were over the Commander, who was already wounded on the leg. Recognizing him as the leader, the natives turned upon him and knocked his helmet off his head. Another spear hit him on the face. They cut him on the arm, then he fell on the water again. When the rest saw this they all ganged up on him and killed him on the spot.

Six men perished with him including his guide. The rest rowed as fast as they could until they could not be reached anymore, towards the waiting galleons . Sad and weary the remaining men reached home without the commander. The galleons left as soon as the men got on board.

The galleons were filled with the moaning and whimpering of the wounded. The decks were converted into temporary clinics. It smelled of wound and sweat, of flesh and alcohol. Daniel was there with the medical team to look after those who were wounded, taking special attention on his friend who was still unconscious. Ilang-ilang was there, too, beside him, waiting for him to come to consciousness, tending his wounds and serving as his personal care taker.

Jonas regained consciousness on the second day, but too weak to speak. Seeing Ilang-ilang on his side was overwhelmingly joyful beyond description, his eyes twitched with a busted face. He wanted to stand up but he was too weak. The pain all over his body had transformed into a dull throb. Nothing was broken, which was a good sign.

"Thank God you're here, *cariño*. I thought I would lose you," he said, struggling with pain.

"Shhh . . . shut up. I'll be here on your side whenever you want me too. I want you to take a rest. We'll talk as soon as you're strong enough," Ilang-ilang whispered in his ears.

"My friend, I'm so glad to see you," said Daniel.

A few beats of silence ensued and Daniel continued solemnly, "however, all of us were sad to lose the commander. He was lost during the operation we had to leave him behind, seeing that he was overwhelmed with so many bolo brandishing men gone amuck. Six other men perished with him. I hope at least they should have given him a decent burial."

"I'm positive my people would do that, Daniel," assured Ilang-ilang in her usual low tone.

"I'm sorry this happened, I feel as if I was the cause of all this," she said, apologetically.

"Sh . . .nobody's to be blamed. Not you nor Jonas . . . nor anybody else."

"Who else died?"

"Henry of Maluku, the interpreter died with him too. We have to look for another one to guide us to Maluku," Daniel lowered his head.

"How did it happen?"

"Failure in strategy. We should have applied the diversionary tactic of burning their village. Out of respect for Ilang-ilang the commander had decided against it," replied Captain Juan Serrano who was beside Jonas.

Then Daniel continued, "there were so many of them. It happened when we were about to reach the skiffs, overwhelmed by their number."

"Nobody had anticipated his untimely death, least in Opon at the hands of an angry crowd. He was a complete personality, very well focused and a brave man," captain Serrano was woeful.

Daniel looked swiftly at the captain and asked, "*señor,* does the commander have relatives to notify on his death?"

"He was a Portuguese who was born in Sabrosa, a small town in the northern part of the country. His parents died long time before, so there's nobody to notify his death. Nothing more is known about him, except that he went to Spain to convince the king to finance this trip. He was a gentleman of the gentry, ambitious and loved to travel. His undying belief in a new route to *Maluku* island propelled him to get the financing," the captain related his story on what little he knew of the commander.

CHAPTER 62

Taking the opportunity in the middle of crisis, this time *San Antonio* finally deserted by tracing the route back to Seville. Nobody knew where it went. Some speculations as to its whereabouts permeated at the remaining galleons. Based on the absence of any survivors, they said it sunk in the Pacific Ocean or in the Atlantic. It never reached back to Seville.

The remaining leaders led by Captain Juan Serrano, immediately convened a meeting to choose two captains and governors whom they should take orders from. Having done this, they decided by a majority vote that two captains should go ashore to look for guides to take them to their final destination.

One of the two captains was Juan Serrano. With some men the two captains went to shore thinking they would meet the same reception as before. The same people who had become Christians in Sugbo let them land with an assurance of full security. Then out of nowhere men with weapons came out and attacked them without mercy, killing the two captains and twenty six other men. Those who survived got back to the ships to tell their story.

Jonas was devastated. The news was a great blow to him who had learned to respect Juan Serrano as his captain. Being the captain of *Santiago,* he was as loyal to the mission as anybody else, a hard worker and so exigent to all his men, yet fair and treated everybody with equality. He was the kindest and the most honest person he had ever known. His lungs burned, his heart ached, tears stung in his eyes, because he was his uncle, too. There was a chain of events that led to his death: Sugbo, the rescue, death of the commander, then Sugbo. Jonas felt a great responsibility, grief, and sorrow upon hearing this. His teary eyes stared in blank.

"I'm so sorry about your uncle, Jonas," the compassionate Daniel consoled Jonas at the loss.

"My uncle was a dedicated naval officer and an exceptionally loyal one. The only one who had not revolted against the Commander," he said sadly.

"How did it happen?" He enquired from Daniel.

"They say that the people of Sugbo turned against them, led by the Rajah at the behest of Datu Lapulapu," he enunciated as clearly as he could.

Down trodden Jonas accepted responsibility with remorse, "it must be because of the rescue operation and the disappearance of Ilang-ilang."

"You can't blame yourself, my friend. It would have been you if we hadn't done the rescue operation, which was most logically the best thing to do. It is lamentable that some important people perished because of such decision."

Finding themselves without captains they agreed and promoted, Juan Lopez, who was the chief treasurer, to be the acting Commander-in-chief of the fleet, and the Chief constable of the fleet, Gonzalo de Espinosa, to be the captain of one of the ships. Having done this they set sail and ran about with three ships left, which they still possessed. His new responsibility having been conferred upon him, Juan Lopez gathered all his men on deck for assessment.

"How many men do we have left?"

"About one hundred and eight men in all of the three ships counted, *Señor*. Many of the men are wounded or sick," reported his second mate.

"Alright then, we should not venture to sail with three ships. Not enough hands to run one more ship. We'll have to burn *Concepcion*, and arrange for the transfer of men to the remaining two," ordered Juan Lopez.

This they did out at sea, out of sight of any land. Everything they could make use from *Concepcion* was transferred to the other galleons. Then four men with torches stayed behind to set fire to it. As soon as they were certain that the fire could spread and consume *Concepcion* they took off into the skiff back to *Trinidad*.

CHAPTER 63

After days sailing southward the two remaining galleons reached *Sulu*, by passing through several islands towards the south. Over the years Sulu had progressed. And due to this progress many Sandakan villagers came to look for their fortunes, thereby populating the once empty island. Many huts now had risen along the coastline and business was thriving. Amir's dream island had become a reality and so were the lives of his progeny who had dominated land ownership all over.

The galleons made anchor to secure the badly needed provisions. Here they found many young pearl divers, tanned, their skin baked under the sun, cruising around the galleons on their boats, offering to dive down to the deep. It was fun to see them, showing their colorful pearls to the men who were willing to barter for anything. Throw anything such as a Spanish ducat coins and these young boys would also dive down to the deep to retrieve them. The acting commander was on quarterdeck amused at watching the eager faces of these young boys. Jonas excused himself to interrupt him with this enjoyment. Upon hearing his words, the acting commander Juan Lopez, turned to face him.

And with raised eyebrows, he asked, "Yes, Jonas?"

"I want your permission, *señor*."

"Tell me what's on your mind, son!"

"Sir Captain, Ilang-ilang and I have talked this out and weighed everything a hundred folds. Out there is a place for us to build our future. After some deliberations we've decided to be left behind."

"Are you sure, young lad?" the captain confirmed He eyed him curiously then shifted his look to Ilang-ilang.

"Positive, *Señor*. Ilang-ilang would like to see her great-grandmother who is in Sandakan. We would take a boat, cross the sea to the other side, then in the morrow we would be running around the village, house to house to meet all her relatives, she's wondering how it would look after ten years."

"Remember, there won't be any ships passing by to pick you up in years," he continued, mulling at Jonas' absurd request.

"I have already reflected on that, *señor*, and my mind is dead set on staying."

He put his hand on Jonas' shoulder and said, "If you need anything . . ."

"No, *señor*. I've had more than enough already."

The captain offered his right hand to shake. Jonas caught it and shook the captain's hand with the firmness of his conviction.

"You have my blessings, young lad. I hope you will be happy with your decision. Remember, if you changed your mind at the last minute, just knock, ok?"

"I will *señor* . . . thank you."

After receiving the blessing of the acting Commander, Ilang-ilang and Jonas went to see his friend at the capstan, who had been sitting there, looking far away, his mind somewhere else. Upon seeing them approaching Daniel jumped off to meet them.

"Did you get to talk with commander Lopez?" he asked.

"Yes. Daniel, my friend, I have finally decided."

Daniel's long worried faced showed clearly what was coming. They had talked about this possibility for a long time, but not as surprisingly sooner than anticipated.

"It's indeed a bolt from the blow to hear that from you, Jonas. I thought that you would finish the trip to Maluku? What changed your mind?"

Jonas' face revealed what he was about to tell Daniel, "I'm serious. Ilang-ilang and I requested to be left behind. We are in Sulu and Sandakan is only a day away."

"If your decision would make you happy, who am I to hold you, my friend?"

"I'm more than decided on this Daniel." His voice revealed no doubts whatsoever, then in a slow voice he offered, "I'm inviting you to come with us."

Daniel was shaking his head, "thank you, Jonas. I would rather finish the voyage and be back to Spain soon, now that we know the way."

"If I can't change your mind, then so be it. So long, my friend. Who knows . . . ? If you'd be able to reach Seville please visit my mother for me. Tell her I'm fine and that someday I would see her to bring her my children, her grandchildren."

"Jonas, friend, I would miss you, but it is also my desire for you to be happy. I know you will be with your souvenir," he held his hands the firmest of the grips.

"Your Maria is waiting for you . . . out there. I wish you all the happiness that you deserve. Take care, my friend," Jonas reminded him.

"You, too. Bye."

"Thank you for being my friend," Jonas left him with a smile and a wink.

Daniel gave him a tight bear hug, tapping his back three times then faced Ilang-ilang whom he kissed twice on both cheeks.

"Remember the mysterious box, Daniel," Jonas reminded him. His eyes twinkled. Daniel made no reply, only nodded. He had not seen the contents of that mysterious box but Jonas' story was enough for him to imagine and believe.

It was a sad parting. They won't see each other again, this Daniel and Jonas were certain - not for so many years nor even for a lifetime.

Jonas thanked all of the rest of the men, Luis and Jose including, for rescuing him and wished them luck for the onward voyage. All he could do was to say goodbyes to all his friends who were left behind.

Picking up the duffle bag and slinging it on his left shoulder, Jonas took the gangplank down into the docks with Ilang-ilang. There were crates and boxes on the landing, big and small, which he had several lasting memories back in Seville, when he first ventured to travel. His eyes met the faces of the young pearl divers who forced their string of pearls to them for barter. He scanned his vision over Sulu, the small huts at the sides, young boys and girls playing outside, natives going to and fro with baskets on top of their heads, who were oblivious of their presence, and then over the horizon where Sandakan lay before them. He turned back and waved goodbyes to Daniel and to all his friends who were on the railings watching them go.

Walking away from the galleon, he swung his right arm around Ilang-ilang and whispered, "You know, *cariño*, I think it was God's will that brought us together. Remember that moment when we were at your uncle's banquet? We went into that little room? There before us was all the magic, the reason of all these things happening to you and me. I knew at that instant that I had already found the answer to all my questions. *Yo te amo cariño*," he said it in his undeniably bucolic Seville accent.

Ilang-ilang drew herself closer and leaned her head on his shoulder. She felt the comfort of them being together, and far away from the angry crowds in Opon. She knew they would be safe in Sandakan. She would also be freed from a too conservative culture. It's far away and before they knew it, as time fleets by, her people's anger would already have simmered down, and soon they would have learned to accept their love at the end. Her father would of course miss her, but time would also let him accept the crude reality he had been running from. Her *Nana* would understand. This she knew in her heart.

Seeing Seville again would perhaps be a dream, another ambition another voyage. Perhaps it would take years before Jonas could see the great Guadalquivir again, grandiose in summer and dreary in winter, its horse drawn carriages, its cobbled stone streets, bullfights at the arena and his parents, or maybe never.

CHAPTER 64

Back at the galleons Jonas' friends were sad on his departure, but they had to continue with what's left with the voyage. Making out how many more months they would have to bear before locating the island of Maluku was impossible if not difficult. They had lost their guide and there was no way of telling if their direction was correct. Daniel persevered, praying that he would last until the end of the journey and be back to Seville. Now he had enough savings for him to start a new life. A life at the side of Maria, his dear one.

The first island they saw on the horizon was *Sulawesi Utara*. They anchored to take in some provisions. While anchored in one of these islands they talked with the inhabitants and made peace with them. The acting Commander seeing that the people were friendly gave them the skiffs of the galleon which had been burnt, as a sign of friendship. *Sulawesi Utara* had three small islets. In these islets, the natives were friendly and allowed them to take in food and drinks for their onward voyage. It was a blessing because days had gone by without food and water.

"Set our sail southwest," ordered the acting commander after filling their provisions. Going south was what they had heard from the conversation at the feast in Sugbo, so they had to depend on this fact. They then sailed southward and saw a large island. Days of travel followed and again their provisions were running out.

"Run along the coast and see if we could land," he instructed.

This they did skirting along the coastline of this island, where they tried to go ashore, for the purpose of equipping because there was now not enough for ten days. On reaching shore the inhabitants would not let them land. They even rained them with arrows to warn them that they were not welcomed, so they returned hurriedly to the ships and carried on with the voyage to look for other sources of food.

Daniel continued doing the rounds with the doctor, helping him to take care of the sick. His spirit was low but he had to keep on with what was left of this voyage. He missed Jonas supplying him with food which had been out of reach by other members of the galleon. Now he didn't have that privilege and he had to live by the rations that the kitchen crew gave to the rest of the men, which was meager and sometimes spoiled.

"Let's see if we could land on that island," said the acting commander to his first mate.

The island was called *Pulau Doi*.

Still anchored they saw that the natives on the shore were hailing them to go to their side. Wary of another trap the acting commander asked his men if they were brave enough to go ashore. One soldier volunteered,

"*Señor*, let me go to talk with the people, and that if they killed me, you would not lose much of me, for God had already blessed my soul. And if they did not kill me, I would find the means of bringing the food to the ships."

The acting commander deliberated well of this. After deliberation the soldier was allowed to go ashore. Surprisingly the inhabitants received him and took him into the village where all the people came to see him, gave him food, and entertained him well especially when they saw that he ate pork's meat.

After seeing this , and being assured that the natives were friendly, they went to shore. They spoke to those people by signs, for they understood nothing from them. In the country there was nothing ready to be hauled-in except rice which was not husked or pounded. So they asked them if they could husk the rice. The natives answered positively.

Then the people set to husking and pounding rice all night, and when it was morning they took the rice to the ships, and returned to the shore where they settled the price. They took as much rice as they wanted. They also took in goats and pigs.

After filling up provisions and water the commander ordered to resume, "raise anchor."

Sailing for several days they anchored in one island without realizing they were already in the islands of the smelly cloves and almost at the point of their destination. Several smaller islands were sighted ahead and they had to go through them.

The first island was *Utara*. In the island of *Utara* there was an exceedingly great mountain, to which they gave the name *San Pablo*. From thence they found a way along the coast of *Utara* itself, and went southward on the same course and reached the neighborhood of *Pulau Moti*. There came to them a boat in which a black man named Karim, presented himself to guide them in return for some favors. Karim, who spoke Portuguese well enough, since he had been to *Maluku* and had some acquaintances with the Portuguese priests who taught him the language, promised to go with them and show them *Maluku*.

"Can you lead us to *Maluku*?" they asked him.

"After what you have given me, I would," Karim promised.

When the time of departure arrived he failed to come. Whatever reason he had for his absence on the day agreed upon was insignificant. He did not appear and the promise was broken. Upon seeing that he did not comply with his promise, the galleons set sail from the port of *Utara* on the 21st of July to go further southward. Four months have gone by since they left Sugbo and no trace of Maluku yet.

As they sailed further there came to them a small boat, which came from the port of *Utara*. They found three natives in it who promised that they would take them to *Maluku*. Having taken these guides, they steered along this island to the southwest, and fell in with two islands at the end. They passed between them. They pointed out that the one on the north side was *Ternate*, and that on the south was *Tidori*. They did not anchor in any of these two islands.

Sailing to the southwest for a matter of fourteen leagues, they were held on with a white bottom, which was a shoal. The water was clear and they could see the corals in the bottom.

"Draw near to the coast of the island, as it's deeper and more in the direction of *Maluku*, for from that neighborhood the island of *Maluku* could already be sighted," one of the natives said.

This same day they reached and anchored at some islets. They named them the Islets of St. Paul. These islets were about two and a half or three leagues from the great island of *Utara*.

"*Pulau Makian* was the other island in front," the three guides told them.

One day a strong wind came their way but it did not batter them, as it was going the other way. They anchored at an island which may be about eight leagues from *Utara*. Close to this island was another which was abundant of some tropical fruits similar to prune, containing tannin and used for tanning and dying.

And the next day they set sail for the other island, which was nearer to the port of *Pulau Makian*, and going along this island they saw so many shoals and they anchored. They then sent the skiffs ashore in *Pulau Kayoa*, and dropped the aforesaid three guides on shore. From here they went to *Pulau Bacan*, which was three leagues off, and there they were taken before the Sultan.

"Who are you? Where do you come from? What do you come here for?" These were the three things the Sultan wanted to know about them. After having satisfied that they were in truth looking for Maluku, the Sultan of *Pulau Bacan* provided them food and water.

They talked with the sultan who was friendly. With the response they received from him, they sent him a present from the captain of the ship *Victoria*. The Sultan accepted the present, and gave them China stuffs in return. When they were trading with the people of the island for twenty three days, and had taken in five men on shore, five Chinese junks came to anchor, at the hour of vespers, and they remained there in the evening until morning of the following day, when they saw boats coming from the village, some under sail, others rowing.

Seeing the five junks and the boats, they sensed some danger, and they sailed away, and as soon as the crews of the junks saw them under sail, they also unfurled sail and made off where the wind best served them. And the galleons went and anchored abreast at the island of the prune like fruit, and when night fell there came a strong wind from the west which sunk one junk to the bottom alongside the flagship *Trinidad*.

On the next day they saw a sail and went near to it. It was another Chinese junk with some armed men on it. Fighting began and as soon as they captured it, they sent all of the men to the sultan of *Kayoa*. They took about fifteen of the men and three women into the galleon with them and set sail northwest steering along the coast and passed the island of Indonesia, where the Flagship *Trinidad* was grounded at a certain point of the island because the tide was low. When the tide rose after so many hours, they directed their voyage to the north.

After making the aforesaid course the wind shifted northeast and they saw a sail coming. It was a small Chinese junk and was carrying nothing but coconuts. Then they anchored in an island to take in water and wood. Then they set sail along the coast of this island towards the north until they reached the end, and saw another small island, where they hauled in provisions.

They found the channel by which the port was entered. They then wasted no time, and entered this channel, and as soon as they were within this channel they anchored. They decided not to go further in until they received a message from the shore, which arrived on the next day with two skiffs carrying certain guns, and a couple of men in each of them. They also brought goats, fowls, cows, figs, and other fruits, and told them to enter further opposite the islands. From this position to the village there were about three or four leagues. Thus anchored they established peace. They settled that they should trade-in anything that was in the country, for which they would willingly exchange for anything of equal value.

As soon as they had taken these provisions they set sail and steered to the southwest until they sighted the island which was *Pulau Kasiruta*, at the course of about thirty-eight to forty leagues. As soon as they caught sight of this island they steered to the southwest, and again made another island which was called *Pulau Mandioli*. They got information that they could secure many pearls there. And when they had already sighted that island the wind shifted, and they could not get a hold of it by the course they were sailing.

This same night they arrived at the island of *Pulau Obi*, and ran along it to the southeast, and passed in between another island called *Laut Seram*, and while running along the coast of the island, they fell in with a boat laden with fruits and vegetables. This boat carried twenty one men, with their chief who had been to Maluku, and having gone further along this island they arrived in sight of some islands. The inhabitants of this land came to see the ships, and so they talked to one another.

An old man of these people told them that he would bring them to *Maluku*. In this manner, having fixed a time with the old man, an agreement was made to give him a certain compensation for his work. When the next day came, and they were to depart the old man attempted to escape, but his plan was discovered, and they took him and the others who also said that they knew how to guide them to Maluku. As soon as the inhabitants saw them go they fitted out to go after them.

And of these boats no more than two reached the ships, and those which reached so near were shot with arrows, and the wind blew diverting the arrows far away so that they could not come up with them. At midnight of the same day they sighted some islands and they steered towards them. On the next day they saw land, and at night following that day they found themselves so close to it, and when night fell the wind calmed and the currents drew them inshore. Taking this opportunity the old guide dove into the sea, and swam to land.

After considering him as gone, they sailed thus forward.

They saw another island and anchored to the one closer to it. "Maluku is still further on," said the other native islander. Navigating thus, in the morning of the following day they sighted three high mountains. And then they spotted a small island where they anchored to take in some water, and because they feared that in Maluku they would not be allowed to take it in.

"There are some armed men who are all ill intentioned, and might do you some harm to prevent you from taking in water," he said.

I do not advise you to go to that island, and also because *Maluku*, which you were seeking, is now near. The Rajahs are good men who received all sorts of visitors," he continued.

And while still in this neighborhood they saw the island of *Maluku*. They rejoiced and fired all the artillery when they arrived at the island on the 8th of November 1521. The voyage from Seville to Maluku took two years, two months and twenty eight days all in all.

In Maluku they hauled in whatever they had been looking for. When the two ships were already laden and about to unfurl their sails for the homeward voyage, the flagship *Trinidad* developed a large leak. The Sultan of *Maluku* upon learning this, sent divers to stop the leak. In spite of their efforts they were unable to fix the leak thus delaying its departure. They decided that the other ship, *Victoria*, should depart ahead, and that *Trinidad* should again discharge all its cargo. This was done, and they discharged the cargo of the flagship. And when the ship was repaired, they took in her cargo, and decided on making for the country of the Antilles, which was a little more or less 2,000 leagues from *Maluku*, through the Pacific route, but this attempt failed after it was captured by the Portuguese and was eventually wrecked in a storm, while under their control.

These events were noted by the Italian scribe who made it back to Seville.

CHAPTER 65

Jonas and Ilang-ilang set foot in Sandakan the following day, and then had to walk from the waterfront to where her great-grandma's home was located. The walk was long but it gave her some ideas as to what the village would look like after ten years- the place where she would probably live for the rest of her life with Jonas. Along the sides of the road were shops selling everything from necklaces to bangles, fruits and vegetables. One shop was named "Hakim's Boat and Constructions." Outside of this shop were various boats in different colors on display which demonstrated progress. New structures were up and houses were larger. In the middle of the village was a plaza now, where it used to be the market place. Then they crossed a bridge made of trestle, which used to be a beam bridge , to the other side of the river. They walked further and noticed a modern market which was recently built in replacement of the old one. At the far distance the large forest loomed splendidly over the valley. It was the same forest without changes in its thickness, the same forest which looked like broccolis from afar. Ilang-ilang remembered her Lala Hana's stories.

Not long after, they arrived at a gated house with a huge garden fronting it. Jonas pushed the gate, they got inside and strode along a narrow path that led to a large open door. Ilang-ilang's ancestral home was indeed spacious. Rajah Cali had made it large and strong enough to withstand any hurricanes that never came. It had a certain antique aura in it reminiscent of well-preserved furniture, which endured years of existence. The roof had seen changes a hundred times, so were the walls, the doors and the windows, but it was still the same home that her great-grandma used to live in. It stood now as a memento to the Rajah's grandiose days.

When they came in the smell of old wood and wine wafted in the air. Jonas looked around and liked what he saw: the furniture, the bow and arrow on the wall and the spaciousness of the salon.

Seeing her great-grandma was so emotionally touching, Ilang-ilang hugged her tightly, her memories came floating back.

"Ilang-ilang," her voice croaked. Lala Hana drew apart and examined her closely.

"Oh, Lala, it's been ten years and I'm here to fulfill my promise."

Great-grandma looked at her from head to toe, with admiration and longing. She said Ilang-ilang looked the same, much as she looked when she was ten years old- taller of course, womanly and slender with a long-legged figure. Her face had grown with her age, but otherwise nothing much had changed. Still she had the same almond eyes, the curling lips and the well-shaped nose. Still she was Ilang-ilang, the ever sweet great-granddaughter that she longed to see again.

"It's such a lovely surprise to have you here, my dear. Did they treat you well at the waterfront?" she asked her, concerned as to her well-being.

"Oh, yes, Lala. Sandakan people are so courteous and respectful," Ilang-ilang was quick to reply.

"And who is this young man with you?"

She reached out for Jonas' hand and held him closer.

"Remember when I left Sandakan ten years ago, I told you I would be back for your blessings? Here is my Jonas, Lala."

Jonas took great-grandma's hands and kissed them without saying a word. She eyed him closely.

"Let's hope there won't be any rain this week so that you could go around for all our relatives to see you. I know you are tired. Freshen up first then come back when you are finish."

Great-grandma called a young girl who came dutifully to her side.

"The trip was long. No doubt both of you are hungry. Meanwhile let the girl show you your rooms. Take a short rest then come down so that you can have tea or cold drinks with me. Go along, my dear," her voice had grown with her age.

The girl picked up Jonas' duffle bag and led them up through the stairs to a large landing. Ilang-ilang instantly remembered the five rooms which look exactly the same.

"What a marvelous house," Jonas commented.

"It's been an ancestral house and had undergone several renovations to conserve it for generations," the girl said.

"Here are your rooms. Or would you be in one room?" she inquired.

"One for each would be fine," Jonas was quick to say. "Until we're married we would be having separate rooms," while saying this he winked at Ilang-ilang mischievously.

The girl put down the bag and bowed out respectfully.

"This used to be my room," Ilang-ilang said proudly. She glanced around. It looked almost the same except for the curtains and the rugs. She pushed the door which was open, leading her vision to the familiar interior sight. In ten years little had changed. It had the same bed and drawers and the chairs, the same old chair she used to sit on, but seemed smaller now. They walked to the window and looked out beyond to the thick forest, reminding her of great-grandma's abduction and rescue story.

"This was also my Lala's bedroom, Jonas, when she was younger. Would you honestly be keen on taking the other room?" she eyed him doubtfully.

A serious tone in his voice stopped her short, to admire his gentle ways.

"Yes, *cariño*. Would you show it to me, please?"

She led him to the other room in front which was also ready for occupancy. The linens were recently changed and every corner was immaculately clean. "To me, you are special so I would treat you specially and respectfully," he whispered.
"If you want to use the bathroom, you can go through that door. I'll only wash my hands and then go down to join Lala. Are you going to have a bath?"

"Yeah, first I'll freshen up before I follow," he said, wanting to give her the chance to talk to great-grandma first.

When Ilang-ilang reached the landing she noticed great-grandma seated on her rocking chair beside the window, looking out. When she came closer, her Lala Hana tried to stand up.

"Lala, don't bother," she said while trying to catch great-grandma who got back to her previous position.

"There you are."

"I could still stand up but my legs are too weak. With somebody to help me . . . "

"If Lolo were here with you it would have been different. You had so many happy moments together. How old was he, Lala?"

"He was ninety five when he died- still young," said great-grandma. Her eyes were teary.

"Lala where's the house you had with lolo? And why are you here in this big one alone?"

"There was a big fire here which started from the old market. It spread so fast eating almost half of the smaller huts on the left side of the river, including our home. So we transferred to this big house thinking it was only temporary. So many things happened after you left ten years ago. Look I'm still here now. I cannot leave it because all of your uncles, aunties and cousins have their own respective homes already. It's good I'm here to take care of it."

"I see."

"My dear child, does your father know about this relationship with Jonas?"

"Yes, Lala. But he was against it. Anyway, *tata* was against any stranger. So, we left without them knowing where we are."

"So you are running away. I don't want to go in-between you and your father, my dear child. Your mother did the same when she ran away with your father. History repeats itself. But look they are as happy as they are now. I hope you were right in your decision."

"I love him so much, Lala."

"Jonas seems to be a nice fellow." Lala Hana watched Ilang-ilang above her spectacles, up and down and noticed that she hadn't changed dress. "My dear child, I may be wrong but I could see you haven't brought anything to change for yourself. Don't worry we'll arrange everything so that you could have new sets of dresses from the shop. We'll also have to get some underwear." She called the young girl again and instructed her to go and fetch the village dressmaker for her to come and take her measurements.

"Thank you, Lala Hana."

"Lala, remember when I came years ago, you gave me something in a blue velvet bag?"

"Oh, yes my dear. How will I forget, with all the memories that they brought us."

"Those golden pearls have helped grandma all those years when she needed something badly, as if they were some kind of a lucky charm to her. She gave them to me as a gift, which I thought was improper. It should have gone to *nana* first before me. All of them, twenty eight pearls inside and they are with me right now. I hope to use them whenever the right time comes," she continued.

"They would definitely bring you some luck, my dear. And talking of the impropriety of the gift, I am sure your grandma gave it to you wholeheartedly, and over-passing your nana with the opportunity was her privilege being the keeper. So don't bother yourself."

"How true are the stories about them, Lala?"

"All of them were true, my dear," great-grandma beamed.

Their conversation came to a stop upon hearing Jonas' footsteps coming down from the stairs. Ilang-ilang stood up to meet him who was now fresh with a clean shirt and a new pair of trousers.

"What would you prefer for a drink Jonas, lemon or tea?"

"A glass of water would be fine, *cariño*. *Gracias*."

They hold hands and sat down in front of Lala Hana.

"Your boyfriend is handsome, Ilang-ilang. I could also see that he must also have a good heart."

"I have never been wrong in that, Lala."

"What is your plan now that you are here in Sandakan?"

"First is to get us married," Jonas volunteered without second thoughts, giving due respect to the culture. Ilang-ilang admired him for such unsolicited courage and she started to love him more.

"That is what I wanted to tell you, young lad. I would arrange everything so that you will be married as soon as possible. I hope you would be staying in Sandakan longer, but for younger couples the place may not be for you."

Jonas was appalled at Lala's last statement but still showed his respectful ways with slow well intentioned answers, "I love to live in Sandakan because of the climate. I am certain I would be able to live here and build our future," Jonas articulated his statement so well so as not to offend her. But great-grandma wanted something else.

"Jonas, don't get me wrong. I'd love to have you here, but I have something better for both of you. I hope you would accept my proposition. But first call me Lala," she suggested, seeing that Jonas was uncomfortable in not knowing what to call her.

"It would be a pleasure, Lala," Jonas tipped his head a little while articulating the word Lala.

"Listen carefully. We have a big house where nobody lives in the peninsula north of Sandakan."

"I know that house Lala," interjected Ilang-ilang, sensing where her lala's statement would lead to. Lala Hana paused.

"Sandakan is not for you. You're still young. Easily you'll get bored here and soon you would seek challenge and adventure," she stated her intentions from the deepest part of her heart for them to understand, without a blink of her eyes.

"Why doesn't anyone live there?" Ilang-ilang questioned.

"Nobody's interested. Not even your cousins and uncles are willing to leave Sandakan it seems they are stuck to this place forever. This place brings a lot of memories to them, not for you," she continued without interruptions.

"I don't want your Lolo's house go to rot. We've had so many memories there, lots of good times, my dear child. It would be unfair to him if I would leave it to rot; it had meant so much for him. And I had promised him I would take care of it."

Ilang-ilang looked at Jonas sideways and was amused at him listening intently, making sure that not a word missed his interpretation and understanding.

"It's not that I don't want you here because it's never my intention. Now, tell me if you would accept my proposition?"

She paused a bit to breathe then continued without wavering. They were still listening, their excitement heightened.

"You will be overseeing our landholdings and collecting the rents and nobody's doing that now. It would be a relief if there's a family member who could manage our properties. Your great-grandfather, Amir, had spent blood and tears to acquire them. I want you to preserve them. There's also a small track of land that would keep you busy. You could farm it and if there's harvest you could take them to the market and live with it comfortably."

Making a decision for Jonas was easy, but he thought it proper to confer with Ilang-ilang first if she was agreeable to the proposition to live far from Sandakan, away from all the relatives. She made her grandma an example, living separately alone in a remote hill in Sugbo and decided in favor of the offer.

It was easy to develop great respect and admiration for great-grandma Hana, so Jonas stood up and kissed her on the cheek, to show gratitude on her offer.

It didn't take long for them to be married. Lala Hana arranged everything for their immediate trip to Zamboanga, even sending them some people and servants to help in the household. They made the trip and establish themselves in the peninsula north of Sulu. As settlers in Zamboanga it had been a difficult uphill climb. They had to work hard until everything was normalized, farm the land and had some good harvest.

Years and years of love prospered them. Ilang-ilang was a perfect household keeper. Jonas collected the rents from the tenants and brought them back to Sandakan regularly. They bore children and multiplied so fast. Through Jonas Spanish was propagated and was spoken to communicate with the people they were surrounded with. In return he also learned the lingo of the people. A mixture of words and expressions in both created a new kind of language.

EPILOGUE

As time goes by, one may wonder how a new language would evolve into the lingua franca of a place. We're talking of Chavacano which is said to be a mixture of Spanish and the local tongue, more similar sounding to the first but lacking in traditional grammar. It takes time, perhaps eons of years, or centuries for it to become so.

The Spanish which Jonas had introduced in Zamboanga developed into a Creole type of language. It took centuries for it to evolve in to what it is today. Nowadays, authorities of this place claim that it is a perfect language, containing the essential parts of speech and grammar. However, some conservative linguist in modern Spain commented that the language is grammatically distorted compared to that of the mother tongue. Their criticism may be correct, actually it is correct. But who had the right to say so other than the people who use it as their language to communicate among themselves? Many other languages originated from other older languages such as Latin. Could we say now that Spanish is more correct than Latin from which it had originated? Or should we say it the other way around like, is Latin more grammatically correct than Spanish? Languages evolve from other languages and *Chavacano* is no exception.

Daniel continued the trip without missing the rounds to help the doctor to keep his mind busy. With Jonas' absence his spirit went low. He was happy his friend eventually found what he was looking for, but the kindness, joviality and tenderness was now missing in his heart. He kept looking for it in some other men but his friend was unique and different. There was no other Jonas. Maria back in Madrid was his only inspiration to go on. Was she still waiting for him? Almost certainly she was. What if she had already found another one to replace him? After more than two years of waiting, that was probably the case if love never existed between them. He got a sore throat one day and food became difficult to swallow. With a deteriorating health he suffered much until he succumbed to scurvy which he developed from having a deficient diet, poor Daniel his gums swelled and joints itched. He was one of those who perished without finishing the entire voyage.

Both Jose, the chief cook, and Luis Mendoza also did not make it and so were more than half of the original men from Seville.

If the way to the *Maluku* island had been tough, the return to Seville was tougher still. Two times tougher. The men were tired, hungry and sick. They were low in spirits. The rats increased in number and food was scarce. Fish abound in the ocean but the galleons were not equipped in fishing. Men had to devise something to catch whatever fish they could catch. An ironic situation when food was aplenty but none was readily available. Algae floating on top of the water were made a good source for those who discovered them to be edible. Sometimes birds who unluckily found land on the galleons were snared for food. But still food was not enough for one hundred eight men who were left behind.

Among the five galleons that set to look for *Maluku* island, only *Victoria* was able to return to Spain in September 1522 with *eighteen* men from the original two hundred sixty six. It had gone out to sea for Timor, and made its course behind Java to the Cape of Good Hope, via the Indian Ocean. The surviving galleon brought twenty six tons of the spicy cloves, which more than sufficiently compensated for the expenses of the whole voyage. They had not been looking for gold and silver as their principal objective after all, but the spices which commanded great prices in the market.

Although the Commander of the expedition died before obtaining his goal to find the spice island, he was given the honor to be the first man to go around the world, by finding a route across the Atlantic Ocean, passing through the Americas then to the Pacific ocean, considered as the most complicated maritime achievement in all ages. The voyage was also beneficial to mankind, which gave science and geography the first proof that the world had never been flat but round and the first idea that gave cartographers the license to rectify the map of the world.

The content of the mysterious box now stands securely in Santo Niño church in Sugbo. It is encased in a glass box for all people to see and displayed at the center of the altar. Its mysteries and miracles continued to enchant believers. Only the Sugboanons could tell the world what they were. Similar to Jonas' story, it had created an enigma which only brought more belief and veneration to the Christian faith the galleons brought to Sugbo.

The twenty eight golden pearls had given Ilang-ilang more unexpected windfalls in life. For one thing they had given her all the inspiration and strength to surpass all the trials they had undergone in her new life with Jonas. They continued twinkling brightly inside the velvet bag, thus creating more mysteries in the minds of people. After taking them out from its bag, she was wondering who would be their next rightful owner. A century had gone by, stories have been woven around them, lore and legends were told , starting from her great- grandfather Kusgan up to her time, and now it's time for her to pass the responsibility to the next heir of her choice.

We are inclined to say that stories have happy endings. Jonas started from nothing back in Seville, forced himself to get into the galleons, survived a tragic fate with scarcity and destined fortunately to have found his princess for life. Ilang-ilang was his gold and booty. Now the story is yours and if this were seen as a fairy tale, we would wrap up everything to say that they *lived happily ever after.*

The End

TRANSLATIONS:

Anting-anting- amulet

Ayah- dad

Baguio- typhoon; hurricane

Baha- flood

Boat- boat with out-riggings

Bibingka- a cake made of rice flour

Bolo- a large one edge knife

Ox- water buffalo

Daú- a tropical wood

Datu- similar to prince or Duke

Ginoo- God

Ibu- mom

Ibuh rumah- sitting room; sala

Lantay- bed made of bamboo

Lala- great-grandma

Lechon-roasted suckling pig

Linug- earthquake

Lolo – great-grandpa

Lumboy- a tropical fruit like berry; it's leaves used for smoking

Majal- dear

Nana- mom

Nenek- grandma

Nipa- a tropical plant; the leaves of this plant

Olipon- minions, common folk

Oo- yes

Pusó- rice cooked in coconut shaped leaves

Rajah- king

Sabong- cockfighting

Sa imong gugma . . .- with your love

Sugboanon-native of Sugbo

Tambasakan- mud skippers that only thrive in Asia

Tata- dad

Tock-to-gaok- cock a doodle do

Tubá- coconut red wine

Uling- charcoal

Yaya- nanny

SPANISH- ENGLISH TRANSLATION:

Bocadillo- Sandwich

Bocata de jamón- Ham sandwich

Buenos días- Good morning

Buenas noches- Good evening

Cariño- Darling

¿Cómo se llama?- What's her name?

¿Cómo se llama este lugar?- What's the name of this place?

¿Cuáles son?- What are they?

¿De dónde eres?- Where are you from?

De nada- You're welcome

Gracias- Thank you

Hola- Hello

Me llamo- My name

Mi amigo- My friend

Mi amor, te adoro muchísimo- My love, I adore you so much

Mi nombre- My name

Paella - One way of cooking rice in Valencia, Spain

Señor- Sir

Sí, señor- Yes, sir

Soy- I am

Según ellos, no soy digno de ser dueño de tu amor- According to them, I am not worthy of . . .
    your love

Tío- Uncle

King Macachor

Yo te amo– I love you